The Best of Merl Reagle's Sunday Crosswords

Big Book No. 2

The Best of Merl Reagle's Sunday Crosswords, Big Book No. 2

For Mike Gray

Who believed in these eccentric creations right from the start,
Who guided me with great intelligence and humor, and
Who, by making my early puzzle contests at the
San Francisco Examiner happen, showed me
that there really were solvers out there.

For Gil Calzon

Our very first, personal computer genius
and a great friend to boot
(no pun intended)

Acknowledgments To:

Leslie Billig	Will Shortz	Evie Eysenburg
Mike Shenk	Erica Rothstein	Emily Cox
Mel Rosen	William Mendlen	Henry Rathvon

First Printing: February 2015

Published in the United States by The PuzzleWorks, P.O. Box 15066,
   Tampa FL 33684-5066

I.S.B.N. 978-0-9897825-2-4

Cover and Back Cover Design by Steve Kelley

www.sundaycrosswords.com

4-Wd.

from Merl Reagle's Sunday Crosswords, Volume 5

I'm going to tell you why I drink bottled water (and no, it's not because "Evian" spelled backwards is "naive").

I made my first crossword puzzle when I was 6 years old and I sold my first crossword to The New York Times when I was 16. I've been making puzzles ever since.

It wasn't supposed to be this way. I always thought I'd have a real career and just make crosswords on the side. I'd been a copy editor, a film inspector, I wrote screenplays, I wrote for TV game shows, I played piano (kind of). But make crosswords? As a career? I don't think so.

First of all, they seemed trivial compared to—well, almost everything. Second, there seemed to be very little money in it, and if you were like me and would sometimes spend a week working on a single puzzle, it wasn't exactly cost-effective. So, many constructors went the "more puzzles" route: The more puzzles you made, the more money you made.

Unless ...

... you got a regular gig, like a newspaper that ran you every Sunday.

In 1985 I was living in Santa Monica, California, when I got a call from a friend of mine in New York City. She called to say that The San Francisco Examiner was starting a new Sunday magazine and that the puzzle she submitted had been rejected because of a single word—in fact, a single letter. The answer word she'd used was TERRIER and the magazine pointed out that if she were living on the West Coast she would have used PERRIER without even thinking. So they asked her if she knew anyone with "a more California turn of mind."

So I got the call, I tried out, and I got the job. (Wouldn't you know, my friend moved to California shortly thereafter and she now lives just 15 minutes from San Francisco.)

You know, crosswords are a lot like life, but I think I covered that in Volume 4. Hope you're hungry for puzzles, because there's a bunch coming. As for me, I'm thirsty.

Have fun.

Merl Reagle

"My Guarantee—Twisted but Fair"

4-Wd.

from Merl Reagle's Sunday Crosswords, Volume 6

This past July I was fortunate to have an article I wrote for the *Philadelphia Inquirer* reprinted in *Reader's Digest*. I've been a fan of the digest since I was a kid and I've always wanted to appear in it—but not with an article.

No, the dream I had was to get a funny story into "Life in These United States." I'd collected some pretty good ones over the years, but I never sent one in.

There was one story, though, that seemed a bit too "crossword puzzley" to *ever* send in. For space reasons, I left it out of the article too, but it seems like just the thing to bail me out of having no idea what to write in this foreword.

In February 1992 I was a guest on a radio talk show in Philadelphia and a guy called in with the following story, which he claimed was true:

Seems this guy had two male friends, one who solved crosswords and one who didn't. The Solver, being a '90s kind of guy, was very hip to the tricks that crossword constructors use these days, including misdirection. And a sterling example of misdirection is the clue "Red or Black," which, as veteran solvers know, has little to do with colors. It is a tricky way of defining the word SEA, referring to the Red Sea or the Black Sea. In an easy puzzle, the clue might have to be expanded—"The Red or the Black, for example"— but in a harder puzzle, it's legit to streamline the clue to its puzzling essence.

Back to the story: One day the Solver was solving away in a restaurant and his non-solving buddy says, "Lemme see if I can do one. Gimme a clue." So the Solver scans the clues for the trickiest one he can find—this'll show him—and he says, "Okay, here's one. 'Red or Black'." The other guy says, "That's the clue?" The Solver says, "Yep." Other guy says, "How many letters?" Solver says, "Three. And the middle letter's an E." The other guy thinks for about five seconds and says, "Then it's gotta be RED. Hey, these aren't so hard! Gimme another one."

Now, the thing that has always struck me about this story, other than the fact that it's about crosswords and that it's supposedly true, is that it took him *five seconds*.

Presumably, you are a little more clear on the concept and it will probably take you longer than five seconds to solve the puzzles in this book. But I hope they are moments every bit as happy as the moment this guy had.

Happy puzzling.

Merl Reagle
October 1998

"My Guarantee—Twisted but Fair"

Introduction to Big Book No. 2

SPOILER ALERT: Before reading this introduction, solve Puzzle 57. Otherwise, be advised that certain important aspects of this puzzle are going to be revealed in the following paragraphs.

Okay. Did you solve it? Good. Now it's safe to read on.

While compiling this best-of book, I had narrowed my choices down to 59 puzzles but was undecided on the 60th. Not literally the 60th puzzle — that spot was reserved for a puzzle called "Final Ballot," which I'll talk about in a minute — but rather the 57th puzzle in the book.

Why 57th? Just happenstantially it was the only slot I had left. And the puzzle gods seemed to be pushing me toward including a puzzle called "Special Delivery," a puzzle I made about Elvis Presley when his stamp came out in the early 1990s. (Remember? The Post Office asked the public whether it should be the younger Elvis or the older Elvis. Younger Elvis won.) The puzzle's theme consisted of real Elvis songs that could be clued in terms of the post office, and the reason I had wavered on it was because some of the songs I used were not as well known as others.

But the reason I was leaning toward using it was that I noticed it was sort of a coincidence that the spot I had left was 57, and 1957 was right in the heart of Elvis's first string of hits.

But I still wavered. And I was sitting where I am now, in front of my computer, staring at the puzzle, when the phone rang.

I'm in Florida, and I don't know whether we have a million more telemarketers than anywhere else on earth or whether it just seems that way, but our phone rings about every half hour, and because of this we rarely pick up; we always let the machine answer. (Yes, amazingly, we still have a land line.)

So I was staring at the Elvis puzzle and the phone rang and the machine answered. And because we have caller ID, I glanced over to see who it was. But this call didn't identify a person, just a place. It said "Tupelo, MS"

Yes, this is the kind of thing my brain knows. Not how to turn off the water to my house or how to trim back shrubs, but the town where Elvis Presley was born.

So, first I just stared. As stares go, this was one of the longer ones. Then I looked up. I figured, if the ghost of Elvis wants me to run the Elvis puzzle, running the Elvis puzzle it shall be.

So, Puzzle 57 is The Elvis Puzzle.

Personally, I think the puzzle gods and the ghost of Elvis are friends. Which brings me to Puzzle 60, "Final Ballot."

This was a puzzle where, conceptually, the odds of success were slim. I can't say too much about it without ruining how it works, so I'll simply say that I am grateful that the puzzle gods were smiling that day. (Smiling does not come naturally to them.) And I wish I could run the "Final Ballot" puzzle every day in the Washington Post until the government starts working again.

But I digress.

Anyway, smiling is what I hope you'll be doing when you solve the puzzles in this book. As for me, I've been staring at puzzles for weeks now, so I'm ready for some air and some lunch. If anyone wants to see me or call me in the next half hour, my better half Marie has strict instructions about someone having left the building. —MR

About the Puzzles

Of the 60 crosswords selected for this book, 32 first appeared in *Merl Reagle's Sunday Crosswords, Volume 5*, and 28 first appeared in *Merl Reagle's Sunday Crosswords, Volume 6*. The Hurricane puzzles first appeared in The Tampa Bay Times in 2014.

I've been asked many times if that tiny K at the top of Puzzle No. 9 is a misprint. No, it's just one of those silly little things I do because I lay out the pages myself. (The title of the puzzle and the puzzle's subject should be giveaways as to why it's there.) Also, I made quite a few non-theme crosswords in my early days and a number of them are contained herein. They're often called "wide-open themeless puzzles" because there are way fewer black squares than in a themed puzzle. Also, some older references in the clues and grids have been updated but others have been left as is to retain the flavor of when the puzzles were made. This is a stroll down memory lane in many ways, so if you can walk and solve at the same time, this book is for you.

To Order Extra Copies of This Book ...

... please see the order forms on the last page, after the answers.

...There's a hidden force at work here

ACROSS

1 Sweating settings
5 Sitar great
9 Meat in Monty Python sketches
13 Camp David Accord figure
18 Landed
19 Surrounded by
20 Airport waiter?
21 Superman sighting excerpt
22 WWII drama based on a Robert Lee Scott book
25 Battleship booms
26 Word breaks
27 *East of Eden* brother
28 Calorie increaser
29 N.Y. subway
30 Evenness symbol
32 No place to be somebody
33 Ring hit
34 June date
35 Meat sub?
38 "Timeless" Leroy Anderson classic
42 Winfrey in withdrawal?
44 Grande and others
45 Rough from rubbing
46 Bard's bother
47 "I see!"
48 Watch word?
50 *Saturday Night Live* alumnus
54 Wine cask
55 Street sounds, perhaps
57 Antlered animal
58 *Animal Farm* leader
60 Michael Romanov, for one
62 Car-buying alternative
63 Messy place
64 It's read with dish-interest
65 "Hear ye" hollerer
67 Lofty lake
68 Goes unused
70 *Murphy Brown* character
71 Engine conduit
72 "Where ___ sign?"
73 Brants
75 Child, for one
76 Writer's space-saver
77 Tough crowd
78 Silk route traveler
80 Estimator's suffix
83 *Die Fledermaus*, for one
86 Sum
87 Vichy water
88 Peas keeper
89 "I ___ You, Babe"
90 Be sullen
91 Am-scrayed
93 Tom Swift Jr. contraption
98 Track info
99 Type variable
100 Meal starter?
101 Cooking verb
102 "I Am Woman" verb
104 Frank's love, once
105 K2, e.g.
106 "___ to you, buddy"
107 Bahamas capital
111 "Randy Andy" thought she was dandy
113 Theme of this puzzle
117 Gofer's job
118 Have a small horse
119 Skating feat
120 Colored
121 Snatched
122 Treats like property
123 Like some Volvos
124 *Born Free* lioness

DOWN

1 Goes south?
2 Dropping-into-water sound
3 Verdi heroine
4 Money-losing proposition?
5 He had a pyramid scheme
6 Novelist Tan
7 Body man Tanny
8 Tying words
9 Agitate
10 Picasso's daughter
11 Efferent part of a neuron
12 Cambridge sch.
13 Little fight
14 Tying word
15 Edward Murdstone's stepson
16 Arctic jacket
17 Iracund
21 Easy ___
23 "Get my drift?"
24 City that saw Columbus off in 1492
28 Some eating regimens
31 Number line?
32 Walkies implement
33 WWII vehicle
34 Extinct bird
35 What you just did
36 Home of Diamond Head
37 Betrayer of the Incas
39 Rimsky-Korsakov's first
40 Deuce beater
41 Want
43 AMPAS award
49 Site of George Bailey's physical problem in *It's A Wonderful Life*
50 Conrad or Cotten: abbr.
51 A very brief wait, briefly
52 Shrewd
53 Swine line
56 A plane house
59 Actress Jasmine
61 Wye follower
63 Leave to have a good time
64 Larry smacker
65 Antonio in *Evita*
66 A uniform coll. course?
67 Runnerless sled
69 Carbon 14, for one
70 Uses a cleaver
72 A Dwarf
74 Period of history
75 Actor Gulager
77 The south of France
78 Deliver, with "out"
79 Playful aquatic carnivore
81 Egypt's Port ___
82 Abodes crushed by King Kong
84 "Get going!"
85 C.W. of cereal fame
90 The Cincinnati Kid's game
92 Status car
93 Draw off
94 Famous
95 Oil city destroyed in the Iran-Iraq War
96 Some oasis visitors
97 TV Tarzan
99 Pieces of cake, for Houdini
103 Swiss river
105 Start of "The Battle Hymn of the Republic"
106 The stuff that drifts are made of
108 James Brown, "the Godfather of ___"
109 Gibbons, for example
110 Meat monitor: abbr.
112 Line dancer, perhaps
113 Photographed pie-plate?
114 Something to share in Manhattan
115 Losing tic-tac-toe line
116 Irritate

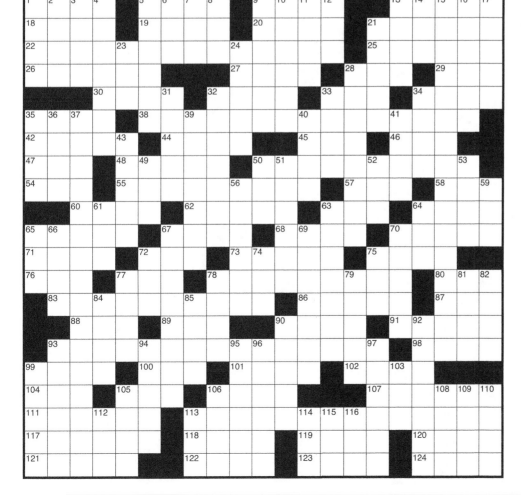

2 Country Couples

...If nations would only stick together

ACROSS

1 Auction action
4 ×
9 Kan opener?
12 Fine-tune
18 Smell ___
20 Work ___
21 Promising words
22 Darwin's ship to the Galapagos
23 "I've had enough ribs, so may I have ___, please?"
25 Acapulco article
26 One way to pay bills
27 "We're shorthanded today. ___ right over?"
29 25 Across, here
31 Feed the kitty
32 *Love Story* composer Francis
33 UFO fragment?
34 Beatles tune, "Things ___ Today"
36 Tinseltown Turner
39 Defense org.
43 A Florida beach
45 Isadora's undoing
48 Idyllic settings
50 Awkward fellow
52 Fenced-off area
53 Less sanguine
54 "I'd like you to meet my friends, ___"
57 Kidnapping "army" of the '70s
58 Hit the ice
59 In demand
60 Stable child
61 In-between word
63 Jetliner types
65 Egglike
66 Fizzy quaffs
68 Ear trouble
71 Ominous carriage
73 ___ *for the FBI* (Eskimo exposé?)
76 Alabama city
78 Dress down
79 Meager
82 Jacques who directed *The Umbrellas of Cherbourg*
83 Flock member
85 Jesse Jackson title: abbr.
86 Can't stand
88 Holy vessel
90 *I, Robot* author's first name
92 Crafty
94 "My car? Why, it's a Dodge ___!"
97 Hawaiian crooner
98 Wander
100 Knowing
101 Insinuatingly nasty
102 Per ___ (a year)
103 Pope's *An Essay* ___
105 Some profs
107 Backstage folks
108 Like a bump ___
110 Stick up
112 *2001* computer
114 He won Wimbledon five straight times
116 Ms. Hogg of Texas
117 "Flat tire, eh? Your wife's never ___"
124 Teeming
126 Tango number
128 "Doc, I've got a ___ in my neck"
129 Actress Gless
130 Enjoy entrees
131 "That ___" (common signoff)
132 Agitated state
133 Agree
134 AMA members
135 Prison units
136 Joan, to Olivia

DOWN

1 Sop up rays
2 *Dies* ___
3 ___ *Yankees*
4 An alarm bell, not a poison
5 "___ hollers ..."
6 Most important
7 Gardner who created a lawyer
8 One of the sauruses
9 Party pooper
10 Commotion
11 Arthur Conan Doyle saga, with *The*
12 Singer Lane and others
13 Susan of *L.A. Law*
14 Recruiter: "Why don't ___ out of the Army?"
15 "Are ___ it up or do it right this time?"
16 Open a "boil-in-a-bag"
17 Communications combiner
19 Babes' hangout?
24 Auto grp.
28 *Nightline* network
30 Brain pain
35 Venomous ones
36 Poland's Walesa
37 Type of committee
38 "Peachy keen!"
40 Pierce portrayer
41 Inaudible, as TV volume
42 ___ *Town*
44 Instance, in France
46 Do laces again
47 Mr. Friendly or Mr. Rogers
49 Trip to the big game
51 Mover's rental
55 Cash register button
56 Before it happened, in Latin
62 Renounce
64 Takes care of
67 "At Chub Boy's, our big portions never ___"
69 Column guide, in typing
70 Pepper, for one: abbr.
72 Way in
74 Editors' environs
75 Go over old arguments
76 Eensy-weensy particle
77 "Oh, brother! Not a chance!"
80 Low point
81 Exchange
82 ___ double take
84 Stretched out
87 Breezed through
89 Was up on
91 Robin Cook book
93 Tuber with turkey
95 Nightcap
96 Frees from a fastener
99 Kidder and Fonteyn
104 Japanese theater
106 Sand bars
109 Describes
111 Rudimentary
113 Green and Smith
114 Largemouth catch
115 Safety org.
118 Wall St. abbr.
119 Sea between Kazakhstan and Uzbekistan
120 Till item
121 Often customized vehicles
122 Four, on old clocks
123 Wee workers
125 Unknown Richard
127 The killing field

ACROSS

1 It probably came first
7 Prozac maker, ___ Lilly
10 *Enterprise* navigator
14 Indicator
18 Hall-of-Famer Fingers
19 Politician's stand?
20 Fossil-hunter's find
22 Tulsa university
24 Clean ___ (eat everything)
25 Shade from the sun
26 March exhibitions
28 Provoked in sport
29 Spanish nobleman
31 Ex-Twin Tony
32 Lobster moms
33 Atticus Finch creator
34 Old White House moniker
35 To go, in Togo
37 WWII partisan leader
41 ___ California
44 Road workers
47 -odd
49 Cheap toupee
50 Acting teacher Hagen
51 Self starter?
52 Urges on
55 Furious
57 Meathead, to Archie
59 Third-place honor

61 Olympic honor
62 In readiness
64 Point systems, in math
65 Eliot classic
69 Composer Khachaturian
70 Sea animals that can eat
   while floating on their
   backs
71 Start of a DDE slogan
73 Witch-trial figure
77 Similar-sounding
80 Mt. Sinai, in ancient times
81 Indy 500 family name
82 Co-star with Bolger and
   Haley
83 Result of a breakdown?
84 Dye family
85 Green land
87 Popular brand of bathing
   suit
90 Tortilla dough?
91 Dubbing problem
93 Clockmaker Thomas and
   others
96 Sheridan of *Kings Row*
97 Hush-hush org.
99 "Think of ___ a gift"
101 Utah range
103 Hide
107 "___ up!" ("Get a move
    on!")

110 Shrubbery
112 Greek letters
113 Shunning
115 Best Actor Oscar-winner
    of 1985
117 Type wiper
118 The greatest, in old slang
119 Grand ___ Dam
120 Higher, in Heidelberg
121 Very positive
122 Slugger Williams
123 African menace

DOWN

1 Pledged fidelity
2 Aristophanes play
  (meaning "The Seasons")
3 His horns are twisted
4 Try-square shape
5 Foundation part
6 Sleeping car designer
7 It's often grasped in
  charades
8 Less lofty
9 Japanese immigrant
10 Of small biological
   openings
11 Remains here?
12 Tell tales
13 Loose overcoats

14 Soviet-era state
15 Unaccounted-for GIs
16 Major addition?
17 Scholarship consideration
19 "Runaway" singer Shannon
21 Dentist's request
23 Celeb's book, often
27 *Mogambo* actress's first
   name
30 Words before *mode* or *mort*
32 Actress's cameo role,
   sometimes
34 Frank admission
36 Central Polish city
38 Humvee hotbed of 1991
39 1984 Peace Nobelist
40 Section of an imperial dome
41 Yellow vehicle, often
42 Element element
43 La Toya's sister
45 ___ glance (instantly)
46 Dashing types
48 Masters' medium
51 Microorganism that can
   live without oxygen
53 Playlist?
54 Lunchbreak lgth., often
56 Bread pudding addition
58 "___ to be in your shoes!"
59 Powers of Hollywood
60 Practice doing standup
63 Acts the villain
66 Walls up
67 Big Sur movement
68 Runner's shoe?
72 Space chimp
73 Cartoonist Addams
74 Leaking
75 Disney computer-animation
   film
76 In ___ (caught)
78 Doleful
79 Terrible age
86 Fights tooth and nail (with)
88 Ex-Congo premier
   Lumumba
89 Paved the way for
90 Coup for a duffer
92 Goose egg
94 Having a growling stomach
95 Imogene's co-star
98 Dummies
100 Level
102 Unaccustomed to
103 ___ *generis* (unique)
104 Jump for joy
105 Ford supporters?
106 Lauder of cosmetics
107 Lily of Utah
108 The *Nautilus*, for example,
    in headlines
109 Zenith
110 Single *femmes*
111 Mr. Hyde's creator
114 "Why am ___ blue?"
116 Cry's partner

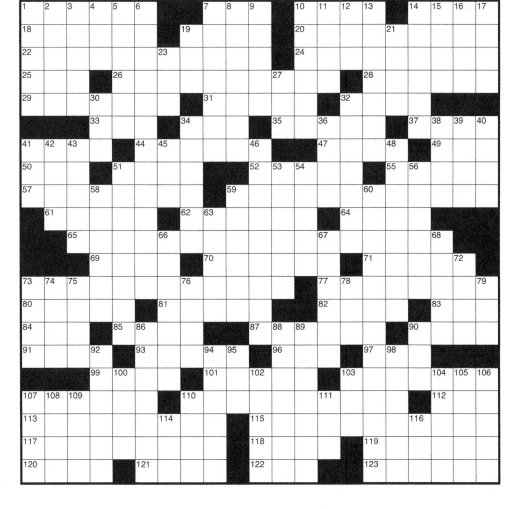

4 Dinner and a Movie
...Something for every taste

ACROSS

1 *Bus Stop* playwright
5 *She* who *Done Him Wrong*
8 Miss May
14 Chemical giant
17 1979 Bill Murray film
20 Gets one back for
21 Last stop
22 1937 Edward Arnold film
24 More, in Monterrey
25 More ___ (approximately)
26 Burger option
27 1 is one
29 Ending for hazard or peril
30 Algerian port
31 Swedish auto
35 Olympics measure
37 1964 Barbara Barrie-Bernie Hamilton film
42 One key to low, low prices
44 He lost to, then beat, Spinks
45 Introduction to space?
46 Short
47 Corrupt network
49 1968 Truffaut film
53 Disease-tracking org.
54 Tangled mass
56 Charlemagne's empire: abbr.
57 Chaser of Bugs
58 1983 Tom Conti film
61 Between ports
63 Bobby who passed the puck
64 *I Remember* her
65 Hickam A.F.B.'s island
67 Proto finish
70 Keats was one
73 1960 Liz Taylor film
78 Georgia city that rhymes with a breakfast meat
80 It precedes tax or thesis
81 The ___ the street
82 Bachelor's last words
83 1959 Gregory Peck film
87 Spills the beans
89 Word element meaning "city"
90 "___ from Muskogee"
91 Pluralized y
93 Wise old counselor
94 1990 Jessica Tandy film
99 ___ be tied
100 Nick and Nora's terrier
101 Throwing food on the floor, e.g.
102 Egg ___ yung
105 Respiratory woe
107 ___ savant
109 Old call to arms
112 Fur scarf
113 1978 Italian film starring Nino Manfredi
118 Present participle feature
119 Spanish salad, sort of
120 1986 Streep-Nicholson film
121 The last word in paper towels?
122 Shaver settings
123 The *Citizen Kane* studio
124 Citrus drinks

DOWN

1 "___ old for such nonsense!"
2 1960s jacket named for an Indian
3 Highlanders
4 Major conclusion?
5 *Serpico* author Peter
6 Singers Green and Martino
7 The bull, to the matador
8 Nevertheless
9 Young Kareem
10 ___-paper copier
11 "May ___ now?"
12 Typical Rick Moranis character
13 With 85 Down, ice cream sandwiches
14 Small cup
15 Restrained, in a way
16 Puzzle filler: abbr.
18 Derek and others
19 Beethoven's *Pastorale*, for one
20 "It's a honey of ___" (Cheerios slogan)
23 Reasons for cramming
28 Capture
30 Greet with ___ (welcome)
32 Start of a Dickens title
33 ___ bit (hardly any)
34 ___ *Yesterday*
36 Clark and Cohn
37 Kin of "bravo!"
38 Drink slowly, as a cocktail
39 Where St. Paul is, in gazetteer shorthand
40 Church collection
41 Putt-putts (along)
42 Part of 47 Down
43 Happen
47 TV adjunct
48 Alexander's adjective
50 "Ready ___!"
51 Getaway spot, to René
52 Next-day pall over riot-torn L.A.
55 Radio oldie, ___ *and Abner*
59 Actor Peters of *To Kill A Mockingbird*
60 1967 Johnny Rivers hit, "___ Need Your Loving"
61 Coming up
62 Become
66 Banking time-saver, briefly
68 Prefix meaning "few"
69 Snake or CPA
71 Holliday, for one
72 ___ heaven (utterly happy)
74 Dark, as streets
75 TV's *Hawaii* ___
76 Operating
77 Octogenarian's time
78 Composer Ennio
79 Wall Street maneuvering
80 Simple Halloween costume
83 Cat in *Dick and Jane* primers
84 Gumbo ingredient
85 See 13 Down
86 Nikita's successor
88 Cop ranks: abbr.
92 Osculate
95 WWII theater of operations
96 Is skeptical about
97 River nymphs
98 Flower part
102 Crime against customers
103 Bizarre
104 Signs of seeming significance
106 Jet alternative, for short
108 Genetic blueprint, familiarly
109 The heights phobia
110 His wife looked back
111 Goya's duchess
112 Industry, in brief
114 Language suffix
115 Had a little helping
116 Kirk, to Michael
117 Mighty tree

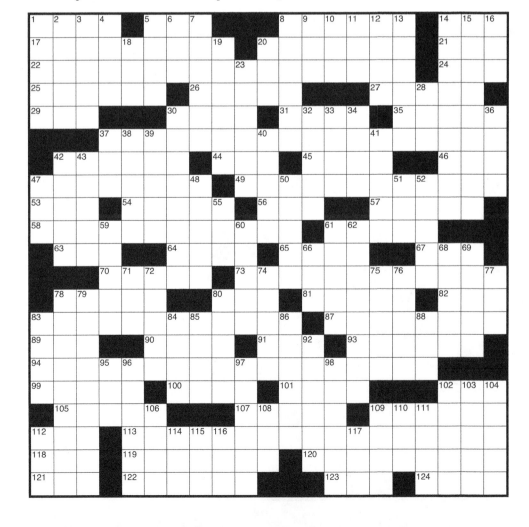

ACROSS

1 All-around greeting?
4 "Check it out!"
8 Weimaraner warning
11 Some teeth
17 Operetta lad with a limp
19 Tennis great
20 John Major's john
21 Like our numerals
22 Director who loves driving old Buicks?
25 SiO2
26 Hit the + button
27 ___ carotene
28 Spud-lovin' funny man of the silents?
30 Tim of TV's *Frank's Place*
32 Miscalculates
34 Audrey's *My Fair Lady* co-star
35 Unit of life (or unit for life?)
36 Handel opera
38 Best a test
40 Walk in slippers
41 Myanmar's mass
45 Director who's into wild parties?
47 Emma of *Dynasty*
49 Point of no return
50 French cup
51 Clean up your language
52 Robin's title
53 "___ Got Fun?"
55 Prohibition, e.g.
57 Pilgrim sleazebag?
60 Sign of recession?
64 Actor Delon
65 ___ up (sick)
67 "___ momento!"
68 Another spud-lovin' actor?
74 Ore suffix
75 Demond's longtime co-star
77 Ad ploy
78 Melvin or Mario Van ___
80 Tiny *Webster* star with a bad temper?
86 Singer Grant
87 Back-of-the-dictionary flower
88 Salamander
89 December 26 sale item
91 Of a star, in Latin
95 Secondary rte.
96 Boulevard lining
98 Slam-dunking lyricist?
100 Coin for Castro
102 Salina's state: abbr.
103 Cracker cheese
104 Least formal
105 At no time, poetically
107 Ball or stick preceder
108 ___ the lily
110 Emperor's dog
111 Ultra-trim golfer?
116 Scott of *Joanie Loves Chachi*
118 Satori practice
119 Up the creek
120 Aggressively affable actress?
123 *New Yorker* writer Adler
124 Wisecracking West
125 Subject
126 Crossword-solving sleuth on PBS
127 Where Crater Lake is
128 Second lang., for many
129 Where 5th Ave. is
130 Dash measures

DOWN

1 First Family, 1921-23
2 Abbr. on a TV
3 Smooth-tongued
4 Clark Gable's was Gay Langland in *The Misfits*
5 1991 Stallone comedy
6 Discovery cry
7 Not reneged on
8 Geography aids
9 Watch maker
10 Drag race sound
11 Clayton Moore persona
12 Bay window
13 Excerpt from "Deck the Halls"
14 At all
15 Anti-mob law, familiarly
16 Computer search
17 Dangle ___ (offer an incentive)
18 Island or wine
23 Wish list
24 Snatcher target
29 Sting target
31 Roasting platforms
33 Undermine
37 Give wolf looks
39 Contrary one
40 The Strasberg *Godfather*
42 Put out to sea
43 Attired like most nurses
44 Stock finish
46 Bradley and O'Neill
47 Cordage fiber
48 Showman Grauman
52 Market advice
54 Zilch
56 Southern st.
58 Northern state
59 Take ___ (snooze)
60 It looks better on an animal
61 Denver's elevation, roughly
62 Hamsters et al.
63 Caesar signoff
66 ___ Plaines, Ill.
69 Actress Brennan
70 Yachting hazards
71 Lose rigidity
72 ___ culpa
73 Where Cape Cod is, in gazetteer shorthand
76 Service's McGrew
79 One way to cross the Atlantic
81 Type of picker
82 Targeted guy
83 Rosie the Riveter's time: abbr.
84 Type of vb.
85 Droop
87 Heat in the microwave
90 Remove, as the layers of an onion
92 Eyebrow plucker
93 Gamblers
94 Passionate
97 An OK guy?
98 Whirling
99 Spokes
101 Binging
103 Chester had one on *Gunsmoke*
106 Clio's sister
107 Mr. of disinfectant fame
109 *The Wild Duck* penner
111 Robert De ___
112 "Previously ___" (spoken intro to a popular medical show)
113 Kent colleague
114 Sighing words
115 No-hitter king Nolan
117 "Drinks are ___!"
121 Ending for arch or mock
122 Author Clancy

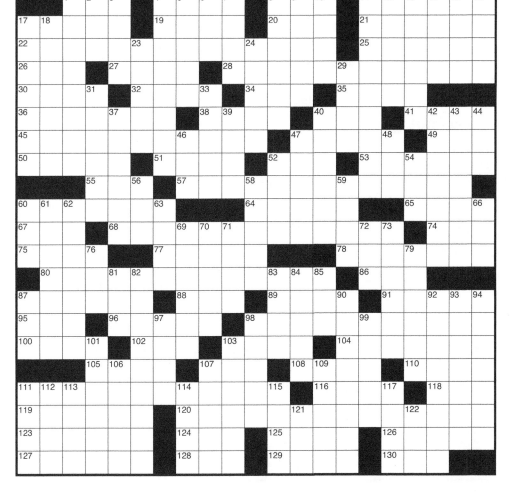

ACROSS

1 Reservoir former
4 Word of woe
8 KGB predecessor
12 Replace at the plate
18 When this bird takes off, it's only running
19 Easy ___ (no sweat)
20 A *Giant* star
21 Pitcher Jim Palmer was one
22 First, ___ all the ingredients ...
25 Daily neckwear for Mrs. Cleaver
26 Reaches
27 ... then ___ the pepperoni ...
29 God, to Gomez
30 Pulling even
31 Deep red stone
32 Fit as a fiddle
33 TV listings, e.g.
34 Rousseau's *The ___ Contract*
37 Elvis's dad
39 ... ___ the plates ...
46 Came up
49 Make ___ (purchase)
50 Take, as the stairs
51 Neptune's neighborhood
52 Ruins
53 Throng
54 Actor Gulager
55 Globes
56 Your, among Friends
57 Monetary unit of Laos
58 ... then (with 70 Across) the usual horseplay happens ...
63 1967 Petula Clark hit, "This ___ Song"
64 Female grad
65 Opening remarks, casually
67 Restless
70 See 58 Across
77 Secondary spelling: abbr.
78 Giant or Noble tree
79 Plane door sign
80 Animal on Boynton greeting cards
81 South American river?
82 A Musketeer
84 "Well, ___ jiggered!"
85 "Yankee Doodle Dandy" start
86 Caplet alternative
87 Sevillian address?
88 ... ___ but cleans it up later ...
91 The piper's son?
93 More optimistic
94 Audition, in a way
96 Hems and ___
98 Memorable Lola
100 Ir. apostle
104 Kankakee's st.
105 ... ___ it into ten perfect pieces ...
107 Overstuff (oneself)
109 Abstraction made concrete
111 ... and everyone runs to the ___ for a Bromo
113 Charts anew
114 Feel like ___ again
115 "Be-in" bigwig of 1966
116 Smoke solids
117 Help
118 Notorious sub builder
119 Desert fruit
120 Stage name of Amy Camus

DOWN

1 Render less caloric
2 The town in *Jaws*
3 It means "many"
4 New dad's announcement
5 Swedish character on *Little House on the Prairie*
6 Wartime prez
7 Tuft of hairs on a spider's foot (such a useful word)
8 In a strange way
9 Carnival performer
10 Make very dry
11 Having a 5 o'clock shadow
12 "Big" singer of "Chantilly Lace" fame
13 War god
14 Andalusian auntie
15 ... ___ his drink over ...
16 Stan's pal
17 Plant new grass in
19 Churubusco chums
23 Meyer of the underworld
24 Scott's ___ *Roy*
28 Plaza sounds
31 *Streamers* playwright
33 Sensitive
35 George who played Mr. Thatcher in *Citizen Kane*
36 "She is fair ... as a fair day ___" (Shak.)
38 Not, to Snuffy Smith
39 Door sidepost
40 Hassan of *The Arabian Nights*
41 Pride arrivals
42 Thieves' take
43 The heights phobia
44 Bird beaks
45 Redeem, as a bond
47 Speed-read
48 Catch sight of
52 Resuming words
54 M divided by 4
56 Show music?
59 Horse course
60 Spanish queen
61 In a wise way
62 Great Lakes prov.
63 Bar or tope preceder
66 Commemorating oeuvre
67 Gabor and others
68 Bit of macho posturing, perhaps
69 ... ___ the oven on his thumb ...
71 Bar under the car
72 Pen points
73 Hot duo, to Liz Smith
74 Literary Leon
75 Edged with gold
76 Place for an ace?
78 Steadfast
83 Academic
84 Helen Reddy hit
85 Symbol: 77 Across
86 The De Niro *Godfather*
88 Elaborate lie
89 "Wherever toys ___"
90 ___ south (a direction)
92 Yen for tea?
94 Crown's cousin
95 North Pole crew
97 Plumber's aid
98 Don Novello's comic persona, Father ___ Sarducci
99 Dumbbells: abbr.
101 Word with hose or waist
102 Mr. T oldie, with *The*
103 Aquarium fish
105 Nods off
106 Certain chord, in mus.
107 Sing like Ella
108 Swiss river
110 Asian exercise, ___-ch'i
112 Teachers' org.

ACROSS

1 Set of beliefs
6 With 63 Down, a WWII battle arena
11 Scandinavian metropolis
15 Sloth's hangout
19 Barbusse or Bergson
20 Aromatic seed
21 Waiter's words as he clears your tamale wrappings?
23 ___ in the neck
24 Noted 15th century aerobics instructor?
26 *Reader's Digest* version of *The Godfather*?
28 Stable staples
29 ___ flesh
30 Overhead streaker, briefly
31 Cashes in
32 Mag that featured a pregnant Bruce Willis on its cover
33 Be inquisitive
34 Sad sounds
35 Frat. order
37 Roseanne's TV hubby
39 Octagonal order
43 Moss Hart autobiography
46 Bass ___
47 Long-time Chicago maestro
49 Showtime rival
50 Willy Wonka creator
51 Big-boned writing siblings?
55 Brew for Branagh
56 Off road
57 Flyer's prefix
58 "Dream on!"
59 Award-winning computer game
61 "You ___ here"
62 ___ Minor
64 *A Study in Scarlet* setting
65 Really big show
66 What men do at bars?
70 Bedrock pet
73 Words 2 and 3 of "Misty"
75 Goliath's last stand
76 Bill the Science Guy of TV
77 White blanket
78 "___ was I ever born?"
80 David Lynch dud
82 Leisure
84 Place with a keeper
85 New name of Farmer John's malt shop?
89 "___ I Had A Secret Love"
90 Musketeer motto word
91 Video partner
92 Cut down to size, perhaps
93 Business wedding
95 Game VIPs
97 Be up
98 Part of ABA
99 Step on it
100 Leon Uris's *The ___*
102 Mr. Hyde's creator
103 Cut-up
104 Recipe verb
107 Classical manuscript
110 U.S. island discovered by Magellan
112 Working title of Ian Fleming's *The Mad Urologist*?
115 Fighter who's always getting cut up in the ring?
118 The truth
119 River-crossing choices?
120 Outmoded
121 Ninotchka portrayer
122 Driving test obstacle
123 History chapters, perhaps
124 The look of scorn
125 Lecher of a sort

DOWN

1 Western wear
2 Reclaimed autos
3 Put into effect, as laws
4 Larry's co-star on *CHiPs*
5 Ate
6 Charley horse sites
7 "___ the loneliest ..."
8 Alice Kramden, at times
9 In the matter of
10 Poetic pasture
11 The time ___
12 Nickelodeon feature
13 The Beatles, e.g.
14 ___ hunch
15 Uses the noodle
16 Dollars for quarters
17 Individually
18 Mirthful McClurg
22 Alamo rival
25 Rodeo gear
27 High country
32 Go it alone
33 ___-lock brakes
34 Sun, to Sanchez
35 Actress Andersson
36 Some TVs or toilets
37 Jim Morrison was one
38 Co-hit word
40 Horror film starring Garry Shandling?
41 Work, in Oaxaca
42 Nosegay
43 "There Is Nothing Like ___"
44 Flower part
45 Hot-tub lothario?
46 Anything irritating
47 Rip off
48 "Well, ___ that special?"
52 Wonder Woman's goddess-protector
53 Hammers hit 'em
54 Warty ones
60 ___ point
61 Mimic
63 See 6 Across
64 Take out of mothballs
67 Japanese art of fencing with bamboo staves
68 Atlas blow-up
69 Ogler
71 Time being
72 Mortgage payer
74 See 87 Down
78 Karl in *Patton*
79 Golfer's goal
80 Art movement
81 Condo, for one
83 Related
86 Topic: abbr.
87 Dame of piano fame
88 Blue toon
89 Part of OAS
94 Finales
96 Put on the back burner
98 Mrs. Alfred Hitchcock
99 Emily Litella portrayer
101 WWII powers
102 Runs for the money
103 Cruella De Vil portrayer
104 Shoelace-tip thingy
105 Zeus, for one
106 Gloomy
107 Round: abbr.
108 No-score situation
109 Sunup
110 Snarl or growl
111 Meat-grading dept.
112 Extended family
113 French river or department
114 Author Ephron
116 Wonderment
117 CD predecessors

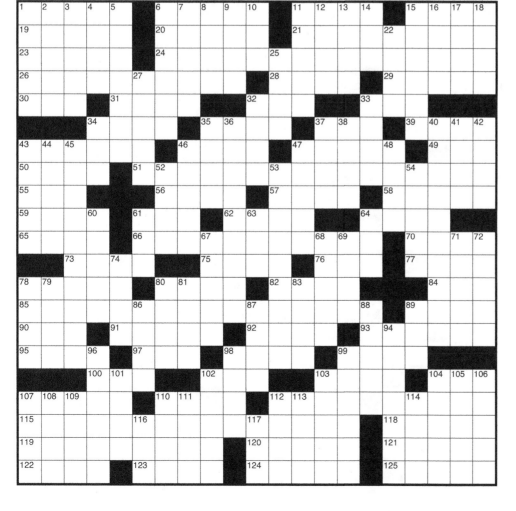

ACROSS

1 CD rate, e.g.
4 Moved, as tectonic plates
8 Of a son or daughter
14 "Decorates" with bathrm. tissue, as pranksters do
17 "Now I get it!"
18 Impatient date's comment?
20 Cousins of Twinkies
23 Credo of the Three Stooges?
25 Place for a bout
26 Extraordinary talent, briefly
27 Speak grandiloquently
28 Protested
29 A god for Cleo
30 The bottom line
32 Biblical trumpeter
35 The bottom line
36 Bedrock resident?
40 South Seas staple
41 Mexican article
43 Extra building
44 Mayberry matriarch
45 Girl George?
47 *Timecop* actress Mia
48 Scot's topper
51 Sees the old college crowd
53 Sylvia of *Mars Attacks!*
55 Doctor's opening line?
59 He calls himself "the G Man"
60 Forms clouds
61 Half of sex-
62 Potter on *M*A*S*H*, e.g.
64 Hasten
65 Puts up, as peaches
66 Popular guy at kids' parties?
70 Parts of spectacles
71 See 17 Across
72 A ___ cry
73 Slangy blame
74 "Rules ___ to be broken"
76 Be a leaver of the pack
78 Main thing Junior's done since he's been at college?
82 "... ___ in Heaven"
84 Puny lead, in baseball
85 Lodge member
86 Alpine wind
87 *The English Patient* and others
89 Screw-loose type
91 Execrate
96 Weather org.
97 Jug limit, often: abbr.
98 1960s guru?
101 Write
103 Actor Michael who wed Barbara Eden
106 *William Wilson* author
107 "Why would ___?"
108 Place mentioned in "The First Noel"
110 Major 1980s tennis star who never won Wimbledon
113 Big fight
115 1966 No. 1 hit by the Young Rascals, "Good ___"
116 Southwestern capital?
120 Make good bread, perhaps
121 1930s musical star?
122 N.Y.'s Lincoln or Rockefeller: abbr.
123 Molarmeister's deg.
124 "What's going ___?"
125 Signal carrier
126 Florida isle

DOWN

1 Prelude to "right in the kisser"
2 Johnny Appleseed
3 Steve McQueen's next-to-last film
4 Made, as fairy tale gold
5 Like Pledge
6 Molecular twin
7 King of the ring?
8 Baseball union VIP Donald
9 Glacier time
10 Actress Christine
11 "___ a drink!"
12 Official Turk
13 Israeli airport
14 Like Tiger Woods's mom
15 Love seat site, perhaps
16 The old shell game, in Jerusalem?
19 Int'l commerce grp.
21 What some meters need?
22 Pitiful
24 Tubular pasta
28 Clothes to be sorted at wash time
29 "The ___ Daba Honeymoon"
31 Soaking place
33 Of a faith: abbr.
34 Winning line, in a game
37 Praise highly
38 Luke's aunt, in *Star Wars*
39 Salacious look
42 Give one's blessing (to)
45 Juan's January
46 Comintern's founder
47 Reagan's "Star Wars" defense idea: abbr.
49 Footless creatures
50 "___ here is done"
52 At the usual level
54 Down with the flu
55 Suppertime announcement?
56 Literary monogram
57 Columbus univ.
58 Card game
60 Cartoon underachiever?
63 Actor Ryan
65 Melon type
67 Rodeo horse
68 Bowling places
69 More, to Jorge
70 Old college cheer
72 Memo abbr.
75 Jim of ABC Sports
77 Had an entree
79 Agitates
80 Actor Paul
81 One, on a coin
83 Actor George
88 Prospector's need
90 Mountaineer's goal
92 All-out assault
93 Mound
94 *El* ___ (the East, in Spanish)
95 Actress ___ Dawn Chong
98 Pelt worker
99 1952 Hope-Crosby comedy, *Road* ___
100 Judge, perhaps
102 Woman swimmer
104 First Hebrew letter
105 1960s hit, "Walk Away, ___"
108 Type
109 Extremes
111 Flood barrier
112 Shirt size: abbr.
114 Michelin product
116 Buc or Cub, e.g.
117 Said thrice, a Beach Boys hit
118 Emulate Betsy Ross
119 One way to finish second?

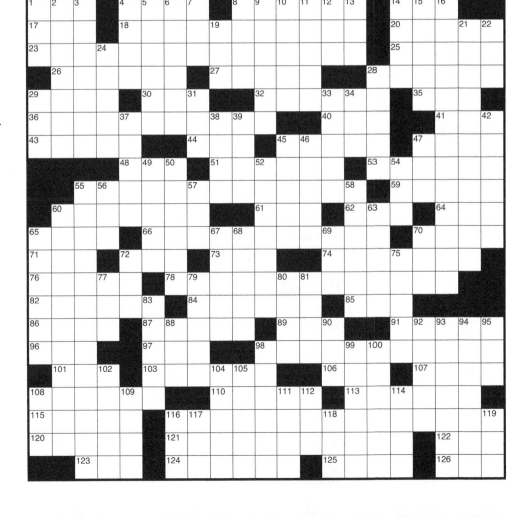

Bow Wow Wow

...A shaggy salute to dog stars—all Siriusness aside

ACROSS

1 Driving test obstacles
6 Metro make
9 *Heartbreak House* penner's inits.
12 Removal marks
17 Withdrawal of a dog doll from toy shelves?
19 Sea delicacy
20 Tannin source
21 Sleuth's plea to his carousing dog?
23 Pick, in class
24 D-Day beachhead
25 Sun City's Webb
26 Section of a comic-strip dog's contract?
28 Viewed, to Tweety
29 Likely
30 Sunrises
32 Composer Khachaturian
33 The mike-and-headset biz
35 Fella
36 Bearded beast
37 Gone by
40 Part of a Dennis the Menace threat?
47 Literary governess
50 Open from 6 p.m. to 6 a.m.
51 "We ___ please"
52 The boss at WJM-TV
53 Due for a change?
55 Of insect wings
56 Joplin work
58 Seek handouts
59 Gridiron game, to Garcia
61 List for FDR's dogsitter?
65 RNA component
67 Addams Family uncle
68 Kidnapping of the dog in *Beetle Bailey*?
74 More like a certain tree
78 Buffoon
79 Make out
80 Cooked but not much
81 Where a hurler hurts
82 Actress Alicia
83 Pop-up bread
85 Took out again, as a video
88 Barney buddy
89 Cry from Dick and Jane's dad?
94 "Light-Horse" Harry
95 A Pirate or a Buc, e.g.
96 "___ a deal"
97 Head of the studio?
100 Japanese soup
102 Halt
105 Common verb
106 One of LBJ's beagles
108 More food for the dog in *Peter Pan*?
112 How some tunes are written
113 Surrender
114 Charm
115 With 121 Across, a restaurant sign that prohibits three-headed dogs from hell?
119 Senate add-ons
120 Bear Dance Indian
121 See 115 Across
122 Baseball Hall of Famer
123 Pick: abbr.
124 Highest
125 Hart and Martin

DOWN

1 Randall, to Klugman
2 Canada capital
3 Flood survivor
4 Tarzan creator's inits.
5 *Invasion of the Body Snatchers* prop
6 *The Ballad of Reading ___*
7 Shade tree
8 Ring cry
9 Haunted house sound
10 Benefits
11 E-mail icon
12 Milan opera house, La ___
13 Squid, at Guido's
14 Rights activists, for short
15 Arroyos after rains
16 Able to stand trial
17 Well-disciplined, as a ship
18 Jazz trumpeter Baker
20 Be added periodically
22 Trav. heading
27 Half a Chinese circle
29 Word on some jetliners
30 Actress Arlene
31 Part of the Panama palindrome
34 John or Jane
35 Wire measure
36 Cha preceder
38 Creole concoction
39 Frequently
41 Bran source
42 Home guy Bob
43 Mild oath
44 Frugality
45 Wrestling duo
46 The banks of San Francisco
47 Keebler character
48 "___ wish!"
49 Nowhere job, perhaps
53 "Or ___ that effect"
54 Thrill
56 Legal matter
57 He's part-conscious
60 Burger holder
61 Old exclamation
62 Bruce Wayne's butler
63 Old car
64 Nettle
66 Antonio in *Evita*
68 Attend
69 Film director Walsh
70 ___ *in the Crowd*
71 Literary estate
72 Utah city
73 Steffi's racket
75 Holm of *Alien*
76 Closer?
77 Line of light
81 They're bought and paid for
84 Sexy women, in GI slang
85 Greek letter
86 Noggin, in Nice
87 Newsroom folks
88 Philippine pagan
90 Surprise wins
91 Gator relative
92 Play
93 Horace work
98 Einstein idea, often
99 "___ from the face of him" (Rev. 6:16)
101 Rhone feeder
102 $100 bill
103 Ill-fated auto
104 Fire aftermath
105 Green Gables girl
107 The battle cry of feed-'em?
108 Voice-over: abbr.
109 Brest friend
110 Atelier poser
111 Burden
112 Have a restless desire
113 "Alfie" singer
116 Resting place
117 Poppycock
118 Agcy. that helps little companies

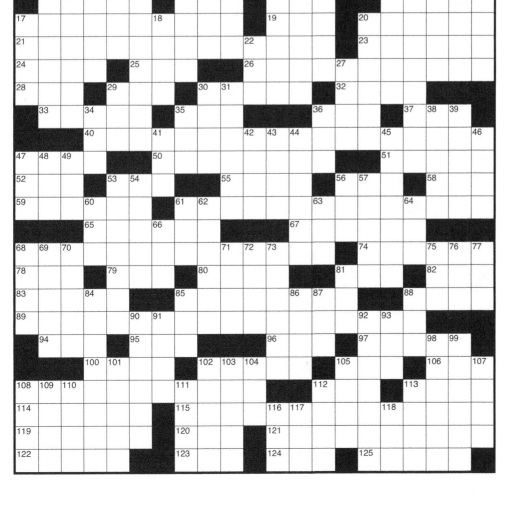

ACROSS

1 Tangy drink, hot or cold
9 Maryland flyer
15 Olympic athletes, formerly
16 Shell shock, today: abbr.
20 Perfume manufacturer
21 Home of Brigham Young University
22 Yard tool
23 Fervid
24 ___ exchange (traveler's money concern)
25 Hunger, e.g.
28 Dark clouds, to some
29 Descendant
31 Great deal
32 Brit. surgery school
33 Benefit
37 Sparse
40 Start of a sequel?
43 Fame, Justice, and others
44 At any time
45 Oilman Pickens
47 Wide, as some computer screens
49 "Are you two ___ again?"
50 Joan Crawford superlative
51 He played Nero in *Quo Vadis?*
54 Cotton-pickin'
55 Message in a bottle
56 Like a VISA balance
57 Addressee preceder: abbr.
58 Discourages
60 Shelley drama in verse
66 Pygmalion's "love," for one
67 ___ egg
68 Masterworks
70 Wisdom's partner
73 Dutch cheese
74 Paper towels and espressos
79 Sticks
81 Bird herd
82 Who's buried in Grant's Tomb?
83 "Ta-ta"
84 Use a peeler on
85 ___ wrap (kitchen aid)
87 Emulate Ross
88 Enmity
89 Insulation material
92 Fanged one
94 Scand. airline
95 Garden pest
96 Word stamped on an invoice
100 Basic service provider
104 Beatles song, "___ to You"
106 A real Dahl
107 Shorten a sentence, for example
108 Any one of a Catholic eightsome
111 Have no ___ (dislike)
112 Plead not guilty to
113 Vacant, as an apartment
114 "Why am I always the ___ know?"
115 Barbie shop

DOWN

1 M. Olsen was one
2 Chew the scenery
3 Expert
4 Scoreless tie
5 Nine, in Nice
6 King in a Steve Martin tune
7 Age
8 Areas under grates
9 Norwegian king
10 Closer to extinction
11 Draft board, e.g.
12 Galoshes
13 Type of cod
14 Grafted, in heraldry
16 Where Brooke hit the books
17 Highland headwear
18 Cast-iron cooker
19 Long way around, perhaps
21 In favor of
26 Henri was one
27 "___ My Party"
29 Store events
30 Half of D
33 Australian racehorse that was the subject of a 1983 film, ___ Lap
34 Big name in spaghetti sauce
35 Tel ___
36 Everlasting, to Ettore
38 ___ many words
39 New Jersey team
40 Indy car sponsor
41 Like a VISA balance
42 ___ to snuff
46 African language
48 Jury folks
49 Up the ___
50 Smear
52 Ryan's daughter
53 Spillane's ___ *Jury*
54 Tourist through Hell
58 Sundown
59 Raincoat closures
61 Hermosillo hill
62 Fabricated
63 Greek letters
64 H. Kissinger was one
65 Get ready to go out
69 Where cats can go that dogs usually can't
70 Get ready to go out
71 Invention, initially
72 Turn ___ on
74 Callao's country
75 Bucolic
76 ___ Bator, Mongolia
77 Christie sleuth Parker
78 Compass pt.
80 Drill sergeant's order
81 Fisherman's Wharf locale, for example
84 Coated, as with metal
85 Don't move
86 Hawaiian tuna
90 Columbus sch.
91 Respond ending
93 Wine grape
96 Benin's capital, ___ Novo
97 Slow-down light
98 "Look what ___ in school today, Mommy!"
99 Cozy room
100 Either Simon
101 Sky bear
102 Atlantic game fish
103 Piao of China
104 Charges
105 Litter's littlest
109 Lennon's adopted middle name
110 Inquire impertinently

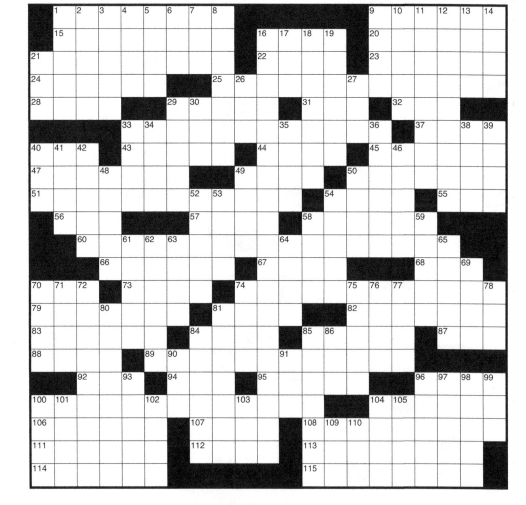

*PUZZLE NOTE: You'll need to add some "water" to this "solution." Exactly **ten drops** should do it. Literally.*

ACROSS

1 Doc bloc
4 Goat coat
8 Border on
12 Who, in French
15 C.S.A. backer
18 Drink or game
19 Rice of the vampires
20 H.H. Munro's pseudonym
21 Show for GIs
22 Eugene's st.
23 Gone by
24 Undo editing
25 Overdid it, exercise-wise
28 Certain stops
30 Henri's here
31 Breath-saving abbr.
32 Scratches (out) a living
33 Dickens sneak
34 New Orleans lake
37 Johnny's heir
38 Silkworm state of India
40 Cozy spot
41 Revivalist's prefix
42 Video store transaction
45 Mortarboard
47 Sink pipe U

49 Accepted rule
51 I problem?
52 Boxing blow
56 Senator Kefauver
58 Diamond stat
59 Toupee
60 Losing line of tic-tac-toe
61 "On ___ note ..."
63 Mud brick
65 August Wilson title character
67 Roseanne, before
69 Japanese screen
72 120 Across's old TV show
73 Comical Kyser
74 Anarchist Goldman
75 Pianist Percy (1882-1961)
76 Pianist's piece
78 Rams' fans?
82 A wild place to visit
84 Hollywood West
85 Former French province
86 Identical
87 Boring tool
90 Shrewd
92 Give in a little
94 Veto
95 Wrist woe
96 Cheering word
98 Bush and Diamond
101 Astronaut ordeal
103 Conformist's adverb
104 Make very, very happy
106 Cool off, collie-style

108 Vintage car
109 Ablaze
111 Glynis's johns
113 State of mind
115 Ad, of a sort
119 Give it a go
120 Connie Conehead portrayer
123 Pretentious
124 *Banderillero* target
126 "Smoking or ___?"
127 Teen idol's following
128 *Notorious* third banana
130 *Ghostbusters* melody?
133 MacGraw and others
134 Blazing
135 Rudderwards
136 D-Day director
137 Murder mystery game
138 Oft-spun item
139 "Didn't I tell you?"
140 It means "somewhat"
141 Part of MPG
142 See to, as a flock
143 Deflation sound
144 Flub it

DOWN

1 Hercule's creator
2 Noggin joggers
3 Some terminals
4 Mud dauber
5 Winning

6 Pickup weight
7 "___ and say we did!"
8 ___ a dog (nauseated)
9 Cookie amount
10 Cossack, today
11 Dead heat
12 Certain stanza
13 Hard corps: abbr.
14 Gambler's last resort
15 Boxing ring?
16 Perry's creator
17 Buzzers
26 Prog. for addicts
27 Actor Connery
29 Solar-lunar year disparity
35 Ripped
36 "We have ___ believe ..."
37 Pancake lady
39 Gardner film, *The Naked ___*
42 Hold up
43 Chills
44 Sluggish, as from eating
46 Round a corner, in Monopoly
48 School grp.
50 Dander
52 Oft-pierced spot
53 SAT, for one
54 Diving criterion
55 Middle Eastern country
57 Detroit dud
62 Party line?
64 Book jacket quote
66 They "have it"
68 Level
70 *State Fair* star, 1945
71 "Good Night" girl
73 More biting
77 Dish rack
79 Desire
80 Middle Eastern bigwig
81 Attractive, in a way
83 Model of the solar system
87 Concerning
88 Well-versed in
89 Verity minimum?
90 One-third of a dance
91 *The Wizard of Oz* lyricist, E.Y. "___" Harburg
93 Like a well
97 Stout relative
99 Nitwittish
100 Mountain topper
102 Cheyenne Mtn. installation
105 Sharp, nasal tone of voice
107 Pets or jets
110 Arnold pumps it
112 Mother of Dionysus
114 The Ewing saga
116 Final warning
117 Aptly named Cascades peak
118 Pearl maker
120 Individualist
121 Like a wet blanket
122 Holder of board meetings?
124 Homophone of 11 Down
125 Clumsy ones
126 Reebok rival
129 Applications
131 Track info
132 Proof of purch.

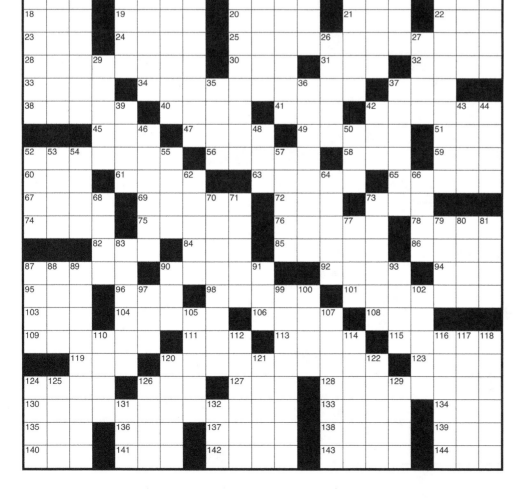

ACROSS

1 Huge container
4 "Oy ___!"
7 She had a weird dream
12 Mideasterner
16 Sheepish?
18 Big name in showgirl lore
19 Half-wit
20 Trait carriers
22 Half a sawbuck, slangily
23 *Midnight Cowboy* screenwriter
25 Drab color?
26 Cowl wearers
28 A president and a Turner
29 *Cannery Row* character
31 "I'll drink to that!"
32 Lab gel
33 Past, present, or future
35 A suspect in the game of Clue (with abbr.)
38 "There's more than one fish ___"
40 Suspicious
41 GI Bailey
42 "___ of fact ..." ("Actually ...")
43 Arson, for one
45 Car coat?
46 Masonic symbol
47 11th century's second year
48 Mies van der ___

50 Iditarod milieu
52 Gem feature
54 With uniformity
56 Grad
59 Pesci or Piscopo
62 Groc. outlet
63 Prefix that means "straight"
64 Many-headed monster
65 Over 30, to teens
66 Supersonic foe in the Pacific Div.
69 Tunesmith Carmichael, or the theme of this puzzle
71 A Kennedy married him
73 Seaman's agreement
74 Early disco, the Whisky-___
76 Do a swab's job
78 Trotsky's real first name
79 Two, to Pablo
80 Gwen in *Damn Yankees*
81 ___ Tuesday
82 Did word-processing
84 Handy Andeans
86 On ___ (commensurate)
88 Successor state to Charlemagne's empire: abbr.
89 Cops who retrieve AWOLs
92 Card in a blackjack
94 Bartender's fruits
96 Young farmer
98 Mystery lore
100 Soothing stuff
101 Forced removal

103 The father of a certain Monty Python member (he changed one letter in the family name to keep his kids from being laughed at ... didn't work, though)
105 Have someone ___ barrel
106 Whitney and Wallach
108 Dark clouds, perhaps
109 Criticize constantly
110 Landed
111 Famed Eskimo
113 Star-crossed swain
115 Shakespeare character who fittingly ends this puzzle
119 Kingdoms: Latin
120 Place
121 Early computer
122 SE Asian language
123 Surrealist painter Max
124 Della's creator
125 Osculates at the drive-in
126 Work unit
127 Hot ___ pistol

DOWN

1 British character actress
2 Have ___ the ground
3 Region: abbr.
4 Old soldiers' org.
5 Miss May
6 Egg part

7 Book before Obadiah
8 Part of UCLA
9 Nest-egg of a sort: abbr.
10 In an unfriendly way
11 Science of bugs: abbr.
12 Previous to this date
13 Connect
14 Make move, as Mickey
15 Hills or Sills
16 Get ___ good one
17 Frequent Danny Kaye co-star
21 Letter getter
24 Billy ___ Williams
27 Dictation taker
30 Where the rumba began
34 Florida Evans on *Maude*
35 Dove rival, in soapdom
36 Buried treasures, in a way
37 Dr. Ruth subject
39 Trumpeter Al
40 One-time beer industry VIP (whose family name is the name of the beer)
42 World finance org.
44 ___ seed (deteriorated)
45 1975 Robert Redford role
49 She raised Cain
51 Musical Kyser
53 Greek letter
55 Reverberation
57 Fancy pot
58 16 Across sound
59 *My Favorite Year* co-star
60 English ghost story writer (1873-1961)
61 The Begleys
64 Doc's needle
66 Youngster
67 With Kan, a dog food
68 I problem?
70 Spiny English shrub
72 Foxy
75 ___ Friday
77 Tanning parlor abbr.
81 "When you call me that, ___"
82 Hambletonian's pace
83 *The Partridge Family*'s Susan
85 Unfortunately
87 1,523-mile-long route, the ___ Highway
89 Some of the brass
90 Encourage
91 Iago, for one
92 Mandela's org.
93 Lyricist Sammy
95 Home of Rossini's barber
97 Franks
99 Temper, as glass
100 "Leave me!"
102 Type of vehicle that sets land-speed records
104 Devoured
105 Bullfight cry
107 Card game
110 Basics
112 Vicinity
114 Lyric poem
116 Popular "flickable" pen
117 Blab
118 Overeater, synonymous?

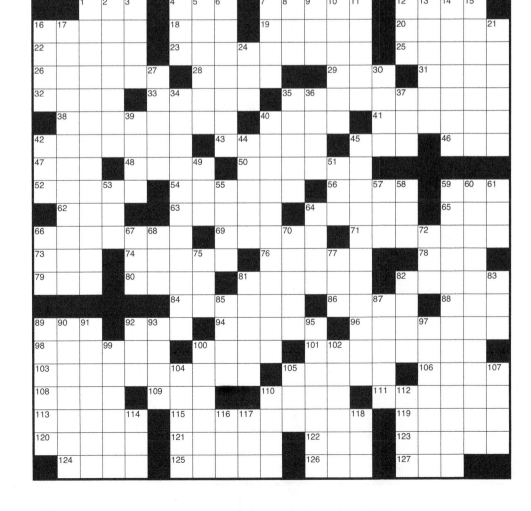

13 | The Marquee de Sod
...Inspired by my old pal, Ava Gardener

ACROSS

1 He's the briny type
4 Type of sleep
7 "Of *course!*"
10 12 Down backwards
13 Burghoff role
18 Very much like
19 Lisa on *Green Acres*
20 Tsar or ikon, e.g.: abbr.
21 "This ___ raid!"
22 Pointed arch
23 Robin of Locksley, for example
24 Actor on the marquee?
27 Hatch out of Utah
28 Boxing film on the marquee?
30 "Pilate wrote ___, and put it on the cross"
31 Big hitter, small name
32 Dee and Keeler
33 Swift's *The Tale of ___*
35 Kind of relief
36 Silents star on the marquee?
40 British scandal figure of the 1960s
42 Mr. Wallach
43 Sound-alike wd.
44 Fail in the clutch
46 Tom Wilson's comic page gnome
49 Direction for the Occidental tourist
51 Western Hemisphere org.
54 It's a rowing concern
55 Luke Duke's county
57 Olivier film on the marquee?
61 "___ soit qui ..."
62 Bradbury's ___ *for Rocket*
63 Luftwaffe stoppers of '40
64 Mountain lake
65 Troubles
66 Mix in, as water
67 Mailer movie on the marquee?
71 Seuss's side with green eggs
72 Who-knows-how-long
73 Paper amount
74 Unnamed litigant
75 Capsule comment?
76 Land measure
77 MacLaine movie on the marquee?
82 Wells's *Empire of the ___*
84 Opening
85 Chemical ending
86 Out of
87 Carried
88 Cilia
90 Hannah portrayer
93 90 Across backwards
94 Audience greeting for Snidely Whiplash
96 Actress on the marquee?
100 A letter from Lesbos
102 Round of applause
103 Arab den of intrigue
105 ___ laughing
106 Result
108 Sci-fi film on the marquee?
114 Indira's son
115 Comment heard while waiting in line under the marquee de sod?
116 Toothpaste, essentially
117 Wear away
118 Santa ___ winds
119 Get off your duff
120 Went to Wendy's
121 Noted rock widow
122 Rise up
123 1550
124 Nemo's home
125 Golden, to Gide
126 Veteran Kovic

DOWN

1 Shocked reaction
2 Hodgepodge
3 TV's proud underachiever
4 Connect anew, as a trailer
5 Despite the fact that, briefly
6 Helgenberger of *China Beach*
7 5th, for one
8 Near to
9 ___-craftsy
10 Half of a French actress
11 For fun
12 Free-form band session
13 Actress on the marquee?
14 Intro to culture?
15 Actor on the marquee?
16 Province of Spain
17 Directors Clair and Clement
25 Horse house
26 Part of UCLA
29 Two kips equal one
30 "___ Wiedersehen"
34 Climber's stepping stone
36 Wolf's look
37 Jai ___
38 Madison's home: abbr.
39 Love god
40 ___ favor
41 Hugo show, *Les ___*
44 Vending machine features
45 "Bali ___"
47 Crossword diagram
48 QB gains
50 Pluck idly
52 Get adjusted (to)
53 Carriages
56 Cochise portrayer on TV
58 It ranks above a kernel?
59 Influence
60 April agcy.
61 Jack played one in *Prizzi's Honor*
65 "What's in ___?"
66 ___ diamonds
67 With 76 Down, blue-collar movie on the marquee?
68 Impressionist Frank
69 Anthem contraction
70 Cain's second home
71 Tired Santa's laugh
75 Throw, in an NFL record book
76 See 67 Down
77 Former Cabinet department
78 Moon landers
79 River to the Caspian
80 "... this mortal ___" (Shak.)
81 6 Down won one
83 O-U preceders
84 Slangy job
89 1941 matador movie, *Blood ___*
91 Comes as a result of
92 "___, gentler nation"
95 Went unused
96 Z setting
97 Writer Adler
98 Bottom lines, perh.
99 Scot's night
100 Less "cut," as a drug
101 Part with
103 Hasten
104 Gluck and Reville
107 Go behind a tree?
109 Joggers' track
110 Hit the books
111 Mr. Sikorsky
112 Tyke's taboo
113 Thug
115 The Patriot missile, for one: abbr.

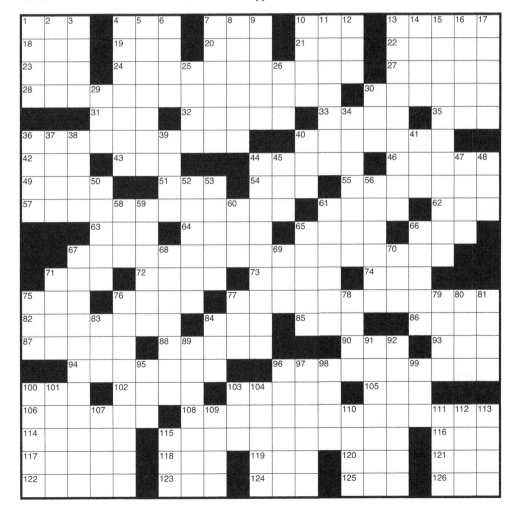

ACROSS

1 Damage
7 Part of a Ralph Kramden quotation
15 Naldi and Talbot
20 Sea-related
21 Texas Panhandle city
22 Make into law
23 Obsolete deliverer
24 Brat, often
25 Sleep disorder
26 Singing and dancing, for example
28 1986 Eastwood film, *Heartbreak* ___
29 Using the same brush?
31 "In ___ show of solidarity ..."
32 They came from Israel
34 Chiromancers
35 Wobbly ones
36 Nikita's successor
37 1968 Beach Boys hit
38 Ending for methyl or phenyl
39 Japan tourist sight
40 Entertain the campfire crowd
44 Sales come-ons
46 Irritating things
47 1960s singer Bobby
48 Deputies
49 Needed a map badly
50 Arizona city
51 Author of *The Faerie Queene*
54 Rolling balls on chair-leg bottoms
55 Stuntman, for one
56 Hit the brakes
57 Eaters with bad manners
58 Train conductor
59 The first sign
60 Zachary's follower
61 OPEC et al.
62 Secure
63 Certain topcoats
64 Cher's ex
65 Pilot's concern: abbr.
66 Maine town 10 miles from Kennebunkport
67 Former *Tonight Show* bandleader
71 Fruit-and-nut pudding concoction
73 Spoiled
74 Simian
75 Bloom in Hollywood
76 Slept fitfully
77 Went for one's gun
78 Hit like a snowball
81 Patter
82 Flies like an eagle
83 Gymnosophist's lack
84 Mountaintop home
85 Place for Pollux to sleep?
87 ___ seed (deteriorated)
88 Invested with the functions of, as a priest
91 Conceptualize
92 Georgia of *The Mary Tyler Moore Show*
93 Have a headache no more
94 Reflects
95 "___ such stuff as dreams are made on"
96 Like relief, in commercials
97 Children's author Maurice

DOWN

1 Did bird calls, for example
2 Word in "Yankee Doodle"
3 Bishops and others
4 They do their level best?
5 Silly
6 Monthly payment
7 Crummy
8 Dakotas and Tuscaroras
9 Windhoek's country
10 Like eggs
11 Insults
12 Adjective on a quaint shop sign
13 José Greco cry
14 Like some building foundations
15 Close call
16 Available, as a book
17 Ancient city mentioned in *Raiders of the Lost Ark*
18 Hasn't ___ to one's name
19 Male animals
27 *Angle of Repose* author
30 "___ is quite useless" (Oscar Wilde)
33 Basic chord tones
34 Unhealthy appearances
36 Glorified
37 Director of many Three Stooges shorts
39 Hovers
40 Samplers
41 "Someone To Watch ___"
42 Close again
43 Pines
45 Steed speed
46 Fill 'er up
49 First name of 27 Down
50 Stephen was one
51 Witch doctor
52 Early release of a sort
53 George and T.S.
54 Meet by accident?
55 Doggone
57 Sesquipedalian
58 Frank
60 Gives away, in a way
61 Live Aid was one
63 Pertain
64 Notice
66 A successful dieter may need to add one
67 They've seen better days
68 Minuet kin
69 Gilbert and Sullivan creation
70 Editor's place
72 Disperse
73 Genus of locust trees
76 Import levy
77 Very tired
78 Carpenter's item
79 Euclidean surface
80 *Ars* ___, *vita brevis*
81 Gave everyone a hand
82 Approach (with "up to")
84 Picnic punches
86 Barristers' wear
89 Actor Stephen
90 Ranking police officer: abbr.

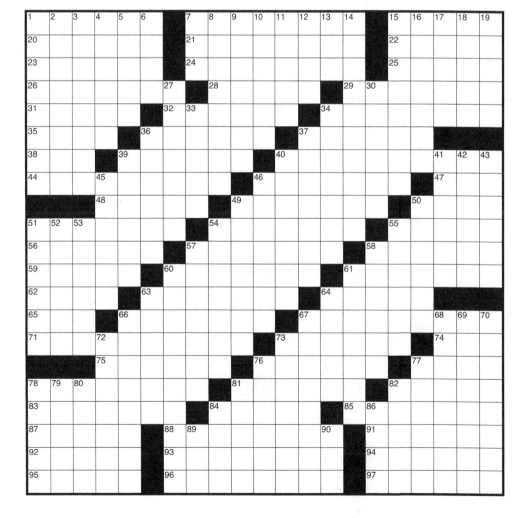

ACROSS

1 **Start of an April observation**
7 Crime
14 East Indian pepper
19 Scansion pause
20 Behaves like a pupil?
21 Saudi neighbor
22 **Part 2 of the observation**
24 Cancel
25 Kitchen meas.
26 Oeuvre set in Egypt
27 Driver's licenses, e.g.
28 Commotion
30 Actress Roxana
31 Hosp. employees
32 Cell acid
34 "___ to you, pal!"
36 Like some cereal
37 *Star Wars* kid
40 **Part 3 of the observation**
44 New Orleans Rice?
45 *Ben-Hur* co-star
46 Mae West film, ___ *Angel*
47 OK'd: abbr.
48 **Part 4 of the observation**
51 Boxes for bucks
55 Hurry
56 Everyday verb
57 Three-inch amphibian
58 Job
60 "The Beloved Disciple"
62 Veggies, in Versailles
64 Back
66 Smell ___
67 **Part 5 of the observation**
69 **Part 6 of the observation**
71 Hoffer or Rohmer
73 A really big shoe
74 A lot less than thrilling
75 Fancy word for a traveler
78 *Make Room for Daddy* uncle played by Hans Conried
80 Stretcher of a sort
82 Pea jacket
83 Sellout sign
84 Double-cross
85 **Part 7 of the observation**
89 Carnival city
91 Of sailing: abbr.
92 Trig function
93 Place to crawl back into
94 **Part 8 of the observation**
99 Leatherworking tools
100 Gam coverage
101 Trick
102 Dictionary abbr.
103 Biol., e.g.
105 ___ snail's pace
106 Big Apple newspaper inits.
107 Eggs
109 Concerning
111 Bring up the rear
114 Wine from Hungary
116 **Part 9 of the observation**
121 Sapheaded
122 Bobby Short tickles them
123 Thin ___
124 Provides (for oneself)
125 Is iffy
126 **Observation's answer, either way you read it**

DOWN

1 Brown shades
2 It's stacked
3 Telepathy, briefly
4 Flyers Jeana Yeager and Dick ___, the first to circle the globe without refueling
5 "To ___ human"
6 Uttered
7 Not matching
8 Son- or daughter-related
9 Ran like hell
10 Comestibles
11 Word with no vowels
12 Marine reserve?
13 The interim 25-center before the Post Office actually had one
14 Florence farewell
15 Final resting place, for some
16 Japanese battle cry
17 Regard as identical
18 Barty and Budd
19 Word with tom or top
23 Either of Larry's *Newhart* brothers
29 Creme ___ creme
31 Donna Stone, really
33 Painter's poser
34 Frank and Nancy
35 Out of control
36 The Isthmus ___
37 Wood strips
38 Not touched by boxers or bullets
39 Leg part
40 Soliloquy start
41 "Holy moly!"
42 Diving duck
43 ___ *dixit*
45 George and Robert
49 Hawaiian getaway
50 Fit of pique
52 Matinee, often
53 Spanish queen
54 Alvin C. York was one
58 Slipper?
59 Incite
61 Naturally
62 Lenore's lamenter
63 Pass
65 Prefix meaning "outer"
68 A word to the whiz?
69 Reefer hit
70 Lady of space
71 UFO crew
72 Caviar
74 He lost out to Amundsen
76 "Stop ___ shoot!"
77 Stop and smell 'em
79 Mayberry kid
81 Malaria symptom
82 Ale amount
85 Abbrs. after corp. names
86 Len Deighton novel
87 ___ anchor (rests)
88 *Dom yum gai* cuisine
90 Grand Ole ___
94 Speculating words
95 Great joke
96 Certain bullet-train rider
97 Beat at Sotheby's
98 Flew high
103 Squirrel away
104 Hipbones
106 Funny guy Louis and science guy Bill
107 Grimm character
108 Phlebotomist's target
110 RBI or ERA
111 Prevaricator
112 Author Kingsley
113 Colloidal stuff
115 Joining word
117 "___ got it!"
118 Elephants' org.
119 Donkey
120 Part of TNT

16 Going Up!

..."Affordable housing"—the official oxymoron of California

ACROSS

1 One-drink, two-straws folks
8 Where the Freedom March of 1965 took place
15 Broil preceder
19 Chekov drama?
20 Stanislaw Lem novel
21 Rabbit relative
22 **With 38 and 52 Across, the intro to an observation**
24 An Indian, not a Jimmy Durante word
25 Liable
26 Some steaks
27 "Step ___!"
29 Court VIPs
30 Winter vehicle
32 Lick and stick
33 Egg opening
34 Where's this guy?
36 Forget-___
38 **See 22 Across**
43 Arrow's bowstring groove
45 Windy-day hobbyist
46 Scarlett et al.
47 Freeway snarl
49 "___ Be Loved By You"
51 "Will build to ___"
52 **See 22 Across**
54 Most scrumptious

58 Think of suddenly
59 Stop, *dans le metro*
60 They're interest-free?
61 Delta rival
62 Phone abbr.
63 Some moles
64 Lovable pooches
65 Suitable for *Elle*
66 When M.L.K. Jr. was born
67 Superhero accessories
68 Austerity
69 Predator (or creditor?)
70 Spoiled
72 **With 82 and 105 Across, the observation**
74 Black, to Bardot
75 He's Bradley in *Patton*
76 Elihu and Linus
77 Black-and-blue mark
80 Count William
81 Actress Tierney
82 **See 72 Across**
86 Dragnet
90 Mortal remains
91 *Green Acres* handyman and others
92 Cigar brand, ___-Tampa
94 Certain solo
95 Area of San Francisco, ___ Valley

96 Book with bulk
98 Cheaply
102 Bldg. leveler, perhaps
103 My team's
105 **See 72 Across**
108 Cut, as roses
109 Lured
110 Open-shelved cabinets
111 Actress ___ May Oliver
112 Girl of song
113 Old autos

DOWN

1 Bread or rice, e.g.
2 Hurry
3 Start of MGM's motto
4 Atlas lines: abbr.
5 "To ___ human ..."
6 Injure (a bone) again
7 Space station launched in 1973
8 Spore sacs
9 Bird or birdbrain
10 Handouts
11 Impact sound
12 "Your worries ___"
13 Gilligan's boat
14 Italian wine city
15 The Blues Brothers' city, for short

16 Animal tender
17 Any place of rural peace and simplicity
18 Explanations
19 Involuntary movement
23 One-man show
28 Low-scoring baseball game stat
31 Doomed
33 High grade
35 Violin maker
37 Contest: abbr.
39 Tsar's edicts
40 Coloring, old-style
41 ___ extra cost
42 Shelters
44 Apr. overworker
47 Clavell opus
48 Mean (to)
49 Last two words of *Love Story*
50 They help Superman fly
51 Nobel-declining author, 1964
52 Japanese screen
53 Crib snoozer
54 "Ruby, don't take your love ___"
55 Flammable gas
56 Eddies
57 Cheap and kitschy
60 Reveille need
63 More like a certain spice
64 Pine-Sol target
65 Cause of death in *Death in Venice*
67 Most intimate
68 Ignited anew
69 Incline
71 Coalesce
72 "How ___ to know?"
73 Serious cleanser
75 Giant Willie
77 Narrowly
78 Echo
79 Herald
80 Oscar-winning foreign film, ___'s Feast
81 Old French dance
83 Lamont on *Sanford and Son*
84 At the drop of ___
85 Gave lip
87 Maestro Toscanini
88 Grimaces
89 Wood strips
93 Celebes oxen
97 Olive genus
98 Geometric points
99 Lawyer Marshall in a TV oldie
100 Hay or sleigh follower
101 Kind of 1960s dancing
104 Healthy fare, ___ cuisine
106 Nothing
107 Encountered

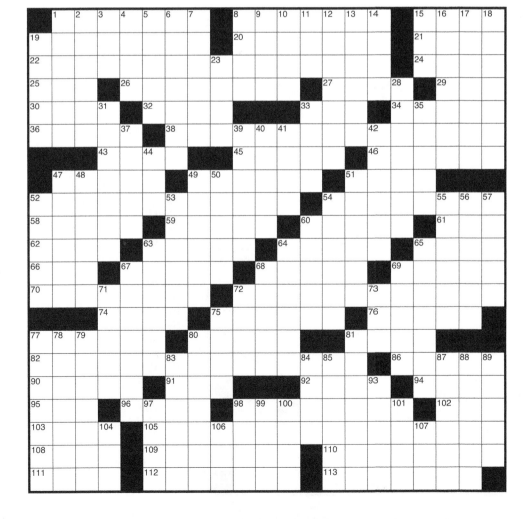

17 My Sediments Exactly

...Tasting, 1-2-3, tasting—is this on?

ACROSS

1 Encouraging touch
4 *Jaws* star
8 "*A votre ___*"
13 Hedda, to Louella
18 Woody's son
19 Something solemn
20 McGarrett's signoff
21 Subside
22 Wine-tasting millionaires?
25 N Brazil port
26 "___ ears!"
27 Full of bacteria
28 Businessperson's intro
30 Go nose-to-nose at a wine competition?
35 Vegas opening?
36 Show at the front
37 ___ a limb
38 Beginning
40 Took the stand (oddly enough)
42 Tie again in a way
46 Sparkling Ruby
48 La-la intro
49 Divot content
52 Dog seen at the end of *Family Ties* episodes
54 Tension-filled wine-tasting?
57 Study for one aspect of wine-tasting?
60 Wine concern
61 Prego competitor
62 Insult-filled fete
63 ER denizens
65 Thorns in society's side
69 Very dry
70 Sanborn's instrument
71 Police blotter abbr.
73 Cut and paste
74 1929 feeling
76 "Adieu"
79 Hatch of Utah
81 Wash
82 Old Brit. coin
84 Pourer's skill at a wine-tasting?
87 Wine-tasting ailment?
91 Bend, as a ship's plank
92 Binges (on)
93 Blood letters
94 Part of "snafu"
95 Wine salutes
97 Like many Helmuts: abbr.
99 Specs parts
101 Mrs. Dithers et al.
103 Day of the wk.
105 Part of B.C.E.
108 Grape artwork at a wine-tasting?
115 Negotiators with management
116 ___ for the common cold
117 ___ fast one
118 Part of E.A.P.
120 Wine-taster's opinion of this puzzle?
124 Prickly pears
125 Belief system
126 Promises to pay
127 Youngsters
128 Parrying weapons
129 Able to seat six easily
130 Pharaoh's slitherers
131 U.S. Pres., 1890-1969

DOWN

1 Fundamental
2 Andes animal
3 Exposed in a way
4 Part of the Trinity
5 Traditional Scottish dish
6 "Whattaya lookin' ___?" (Lou Costello cry)
7 San Francisco feature
8 VCR maker
9 Tuskegee's st.
10 End of a Chevy Chase intro
11 Museum or opera house
12 No problem
13 Morocco's capital
14 Spain and Portugal
15 S Georgia college city
16 Satisfied a craving
17 Author Stanislaw
18 Relative of "get real," in *Clueless*
23 They, in Tours
24 Big name in U.S. trucks
29 Place to see stars?
31 Snickers et al.
32 Ridiculed
33 Pig meat, in 59 Down
34 *Cheers* regular
39 Watcher of the skies: abbr.
41 Razor-billed bird
43 Old French coins
44 Trent of Mississippi
45 Technique, to Tiberius
47 Don't lean too far over it
49 Seat belt
50 Tara belle
51 Start eating
53 Wolfpack member
55 Gold-painted statuettes
56 Mardi Gras and Carnival
58 One with clothes-trophobia?
59 Mexican state
64 Glides over the surface of
66 Northwestern state
67 In a rage
68 Hitchcock's 39
72 Neil Sedaka hit, "Next Door to ___"
75 Fizzy drink
77 Rat-a-___
78 Melodic, in music
79 "Just the two ___"
80 Excellent, on Tin Pan Alley
83 Modern fastener
85 Muslim title
86 One of Steve Allen's "men on the street"
87 Place to hoist a few
88 Final announcement?
89 *Amadeus* star
90 Flatfish
96 Music machines
98 Construct anew
100 Mr. Smith's body?
102 ___ the occasion
104 Exhausts
106 Prepare for more shooting
107 Refer (to)
109 The End
110 Tickle one's ___
111 Supreme Ct. convening mo.
112 Ancient land along the Nile
113 It's payback time: abbr.
114 Smart talk
118 Deck leader
119 Luxury locale
121 Comedienne Margaret
122 Toothpaste brand
123 Lion's tail?

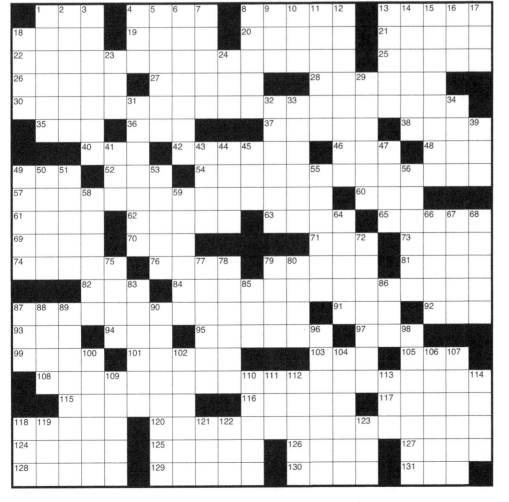

18 | Yesterday I Looked Out a Cafe Window and Saw ...

ACROSS

1 Police officers
7 Prairie product
12 Mayberry's perennial self-incarcerator
16 Terhune pooch
19 "Forget it!"
20 Oprah's aptly named production company
21 *La* ___ (Beijing's land, in Italian)
22 Film editors' org.
23 **A 1948 film**
26 The sow palace?
27 N to the zeroth power
28 Sermon topic
29 Like a cold day in hell
30 Type of solvent, briefly
32 **A 1981 film**
37 Erstwhile anesthetic
41 Overacts
42 Attila, to his wife?
43 More like a toon
46 Agro or astro ending
47 Port of Spain's island
52 **A 1990 film**
54 **A 1987 film**
55 Renaissance Fair adjective
56 Medical grp.
57 Dagger's companion

58 Where John Wooden coached
59 **A 1987 film**
61 Timber-hewing tool
65 Take to court
67 Some golfers: abbr.
68 **A 1975 film**
72 Suspend, to a Cockney
75 Hades, to a Cockney
76 More minuscule
77 **A 1967 film**
79 Kin of FYI
82 In ___ (worried)
85 Uncooked
87 ___ bone to pick
88 **A 1981 film**
90 **A 1938 film**
94 Anagram of LABOR DAY
95 Latin abbr.
96 Germ-free
97 Lemon drink
98 Choreographer Alonso
100 Surgery tool
101 **A 1953 film**
107 Says, in teenspeak
108 Fishing need
109 Bachelorhood adieu
110 The bride
113 Start of a Remarque classic
114 **A 1950 film**

121 Part of the i
122 Not "fer"
123 Sunni reading
124 Mexican state
125 Slangy coffee
126 Supports for Couples
127 Out doors
128 Blues partner

DOWN

1 Boom stuff
2 Hostess cake
3 Actress Barbara
4 Magazine or cereal
5 Pressure preceder
6 Like a corgi
7 Evan Hunter novel, *Strangers ___ Meet*
8 Piece of sardonic laughter
9 Tarzan creator's inits.
10 Car loan abbr.
11 Competition, in brief
12 Earth hue, to an earl
13 Watch company
14 Balin or Claire
15 Sahara sight
16 Will Rogers prop
17 Sheen or Short
18 Actress Susan
24 Baldfaced item

25 Lacking
31 French girl's name
32 The Limeliters were one
33 Present opener?
34 The Baskervilles' backyard
35 "Don't look ___!"
36 "Really?"
37 Keep these off the table
38 Hard worker
39 Moving crowds
40 Wound (up)
44 Alfonso's queen
45 One-man-army of filmdom
47 The way, in Chinese
48 Essential cell component
49 Prize decliner, Le ___ Tho
50 Afflict
51 Noted molecule
53 Suspicious
54 Four years before the Norman Conquest
57 Lyricist Sammy
60 Gal of song
62 Actor Warren
63 Turn over ___ leaf
64 Gen.-turned-pres.
66 "Guh-ross!"
69 Blew a secret
70 Withered
71 W.C. Fields exclamations
72 Some video games
73 Maker of Quik
74 Starsky portrayer
75 Fix in the mind
78 Catherine or Maureen
79 Get ___ for effort
80 EMK, familiarly
81 Uxmal uncle
83 Sonora sun
84 Apply oneself
86 27th pres.
89 Quarreled, newlywed-style
90 Begin to wake
91 Texas city
92 Removal: abbr.
93 More than one moray
95 Gnomish
98 "Wait just ___"
99 City on the Somme
101 Dome home
102 *The Prince of Tides* nominee
103 Banks or Ford
104 Buckboard controls
105 Notices in the paper
106 Spinner, in either direction
110 Like Sharon Stone
111 Microwave
112 Fix in the mind
113 Pt. of speech
115 Aquarius, for one
116 Roman goddess of night
117 Three in the front?
118 Sunlight shield
119 Cheer
120 *Cheers* guy

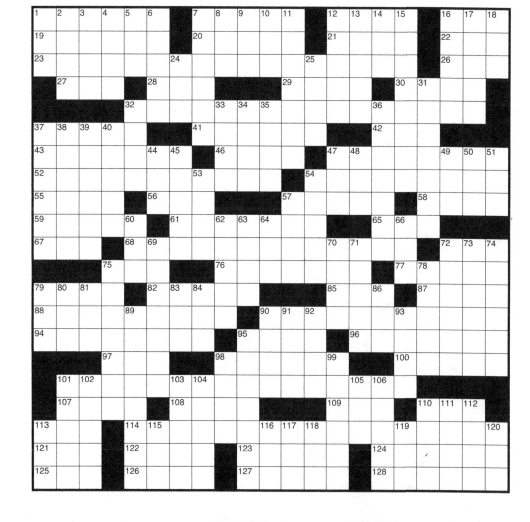

19 Why We Don't Go to Salad Bars with Ed

ACROSS

1 "It's a deal"
4 Gentle as ___
9 Mar. honoree
14 Response to a cad
18 Quarterback's pass, completed or not: abbr.
19 Sargent's daughter
20 John le Carré's birthplace, ___, England
21 In one piece
22 **At the front of the salad bar line, Ed says, "___?"**
24 Oscar org.
25 Martin's partner
26 Eur. nation (with "the")
27 **At the end of the salad bar line, Ed says, "___ ..." (continues at 36 Across)**
30 Floodgates
32 Change completely
33 Cherry's place
35 Witnessed
36 **See 27 Across**
40 Opens a door, in a way
44 Colon opening?
45 Like tearjerker attendees
46 Palindromic celeb
49 Bible preposition
50 Writer Fallaci
52 Coll. football division
53 **"Oops," Ed says, "I forgot my ___!"**
58 Big name in chips
60 Polonius hides behind one
61 Strap
62 He had a head of steam?
64 Part of a Latin trio
68 **After eating for an hour, Ed says, "___; let's pay the waitress and go"**
73 Name in Hirschfeld's art
74 Pocket money
75 Restaurateur Toots
76 Bald-headed bird's home
77 Surrealist Joan
79 **So as soon as he ___ ...**
82 Missile type: abbr.
85 Beauty-Mist pantyhose model, once
88 Indian nursemaid
89 Fabi of racing
90 Course load
92 "How ___, doc?"
93 More suspicious
96 **... he tells us all to "___ ..." (continues at 107 Across)**
99 Painter Cézanne
102 William Wharton novel made into a 1984 film
103 Character actor O'Malley
104 Al's favorite material, on *Home Improvement*
107 **See 96 Across**
112 Sky bear
113 Petty person
115 Weaver shocker
116 **And as soon as she arrives at our table, Ed always says, "___!" And that's why we don't go to salad bars with Ed.**
118 Unleashes
119 Wash cycle
120 Painter of water lilies
121 The Jazz, for one
122 Journalist Bernstein
123 Big Hollywood union: abbr.
124 Cracker spreads
125 German article

DOWN

1 Tired responses
2 Waters and others
3 Monument
4 Certain radios
5 Big dipper
6 Zodiac sign
7 Spray
8 Bit of Thai currency
9 Having gaps
10 1940 Mickey Rooney bio pic, *Young ___*
11 Visits, in a way
12 Jai ___
13 T / F sheet
14 ___ ropes (train)
15 Bass output
16 Where the Tombigbee R. flows
17 Signer's need
21 DO NOT ENTER relative
23 Vietnam president, 1967-75
28 Coffee containers
29 "___ know you?"
31 MSNBC rival
34 Prop for Norman Rockwell
36 Epic poems
37 Int'l licensing org.
38 Name of many a theater
39 Woody's favorite place, familiarly
41 Heston role
42 King Kong abductee Darrow
43 "Feed a cold, ___ a ..."
46 ___ in the neck
47 *La Traviata* composer
48 Workroom wear
51 Defense org.
54 Intl. air carrier
55 39 Down time
56 Jimmy's *Vertigo* co-star
57 "Made ___"
59 *The Crucible* setting
62 "According to whom?"
63 Layouts
65 It may get you a raise
66 Film title with *Mess* or *Madness*
67 Saurus starter
69 Hour, to Hernando
70 Aimless one's state of mind
71 That girl
72 Long March leader
78 Privileged few
79 Jack Benny trait
80 Cheery word?
81 Greek letter
82 Big ___, Calif.
83 Condescending one
84 Copycat
86 Transportation for Jesus
87 "___ is jumpin'!"
91 North Carolinian
93 Social event
94 Agcy. that really cleans up
95 Accumulated, as a bill
97 "Hi ho, Steverino" utterer
98 Raquel's daughter
100 Gathering dust, as books
101 *Gil Blas* author
104 Barely audible
105 French school
106 Surgery boon
108 Delhi dress
109 Charles Lamb's pseudonym
110 Dudley Do-Right's outfit: abbr.
111 A word to Nellie
113 He's in the army now: abbr.
114 George's brother
117 Horses for G. Kasparov

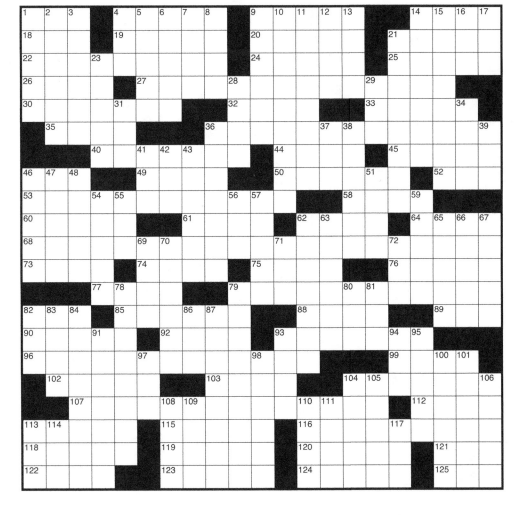

...Sounds like funny business to me

ACROSS

1 Dumbstruck
6 "Proud" guys
11 Bottom layer
15 Healthcare prefix
19 Avis, to Hertz
20 Singer Turner's autobio
21 *Let Us Now Praise Famous Men* author
22 A brother Karamazov
23 The ___ (name for a hofbrau?)
25 The ___ (name for a butcher shop?)
27 Auction declaration
28 The ___ (name for a tanning salon?)
30 The dog on *Frasier*
31 Simian, for short
33 Composer Satie
34 Go over again, as a line
35 Elite squad
38 Presbyterian officer
41 Omit, as a syllable
43 Shake like ___
44 Snick-or-___ (machete)
45 Name for a fast-food joint?
49 + : abbr.
50 Geo. Lucas alma mater
52 Stiller married her
55 Earth's beginning?
56 Acapulco aunt

57 The ___ (name for a pet shop?)
60 Space vehicle
62 Ferry island
64 Singing brother who went solo
66 *On the Road* guy
68 N.Y. neighbor
69 Works like a fax machine
72 The ___ (name for a binoculars store?)
74 Complicated, as a breakup
75 Word in Robin exclamations
76 Tubby water animals
77 Long-haired bird dog
79 "Give ___ a few"
81 Hellish fellow
83 The ___ (name for a bar that shows *Hee Haw* reruns?)
87 The end ___ perfect day
88 Rock concert sufferer?
90 Scowl or frown
92 Schwarz of toys
93 Selma's home: abbr.
94 Name for a shop owned by two guys?
97 Love nest falling-out
99 Chicken choice
101 Rolls' colleague
102 Blood of the gods
104 Of musical sounds
105 Able to get around
108 Actress Turner
110 Farm refrain

113 Certain Arab
114 The ___ (name for a Chinese eatery?)
117 With 40 Down, immersed
121 The ___ (name for a Spanish Inquisition museum?)
123 The ___ (name for a lingerie boutique?)
125 Comic strip created by Jeff MacNelly
126 Approximately
127 Part of WASP
128 Some tests
129 Brooklyn Bridge's river
130 Hammer part
131 Darn that hole again
132 Prelude to porosis

DOWN

1 Barks heard by Annie
2 Airplane/copter hybrid
3 Of grandparents
4 Notorious box opener
5 Antlered one
6 Galileo, by birth
7 RFK's post, under JFK
8 Moe's missiles
9 Have ___ (know somebody)
10 South Carolina river
11 "One Planet, One People" group

12 Blow ___
13 Religious faction
14 Rodent reviler's cry
15 Erred in sketching
16 Outwit, as a posse
17 Roman province that became Romania
18 Signed
24 New Deal agcy.
26 "They ___ a physician, but they are sick" (Matt. 9:12)
29 Yossarian's roommate
32 Tax returns?
34 Most mature
35 Daisy Mae's drawer
36 Shampoo ingredient
37 Children, and children's children: abbr.
39 Moon lander
40 See 117 Across
42 Break a ___
44 Shrimp in garlic
45 Native Israelis
46 Klemperer and Kruger
47 Legal claims on property
48 Jong's Hackabout-Jones
51 Splashy resort
53 The ___ (name for Noah's carpentry shop?)
54 Debauchee
58 African nation
59 Sheds tears
61 Canvas mount
63 Sour
65 Flower parts
67 Exonerate
69 Vibrated
70 Greek island
71 Knot-tying spot
73 Japanese stringed instrument
74 Amahl's creator
76 Old call for attention
78 An airline
80 *thirtysomething* star
82 Belg. neighbor (with "the")
84 Kelly sang in it
85 Ms. Korbut
86 He starred in TV's *Wiseguy*
89 Mythical avian
91 Carnival city
95 Gewgaw
96 Exterminate nits
98 Sun spot?
100 Rug makers
102 Holiday, for one
103 Reagan's Weinberger
105 Code name?
106 Mutual of ___
107 Salad bar nuggets
109 Soap Box Derby city
111 "No need to tell me"
112 Double curve
114 Sported
115 Fork point
116 Gerund finishers
118 Uncluttered
119 Perry's creator
120 Exxon, before
122 Porter's "You're the ___"
124 Bally follower

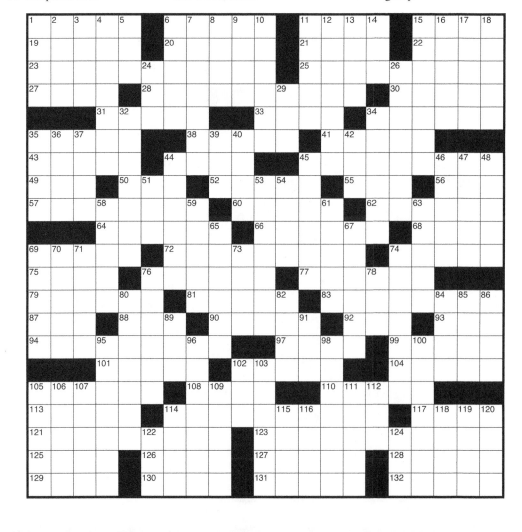

PUZZLE NOTE: *All theme answers in this puzzle were uttered by radio and TV newscasters in Los Angeles.*

ACROSS

1 Site or meter preceder
5 Smatterings of smoke
10 Joanne LaCock's stage name
13 The Hurricanes' st.
16 Corner-window VIP
17 Mortar's mate
18 **Wedding ceremony**
21 **Prime mover on the cuisine scene**
23 *****
25 Kohl's one
26 Bean covering?
27 Bennett or Curtis
28 Slick material
29 **Sporting event**
32 Actress or fighter
33 Luck or Macbeth
34 Part of S & L: abbr.
35 Chow
36 **"The list goes on"**
40 **In all likelihood**
43 Print-job error
44 Late pinup painter in *Playboy*
48 World War II battle zone
50 Some deliveries
51 **Six feet, two inches, e.g.**
52 ___ of wills
53 Heavyweight sport?
55 Rare bill
57 "Spiffy!"
58 "The past ___ foreign country ..."
60 Believers in Hel and Frigg
63 Periods of note
65 Woody's home, for short
66 Ford or Lincoln: abbr.
69 **Animal doctors**
72 Get warm
73 Rocket fuel, briefly
74 Irene Cara film
75 Chocolate people
76 Noted democracy of mostly non-voters
78 Open-mouthed
80 "Mischievious" one
82 Prudhomme, for one
84 "___ all a good night"
88 **Type of energy**
90 Singer McEntire
93 Drink
95 Popular video game
96 Status auto
97 **A month**
98 **Cafe order**
100 Late purveyor of "Herb asides," in San Francisco
102 Negligent
103 Air force?
106 Put away groceries?
107 **Crowning blow**
111 Gessler's canton
112 First name in perfume
114 Worthless writing
115 Italian car
116 **Fever symptom**
119 **Like America's pronunciation**
123 **A continent**
124 "We ___ amused"
125 "What's ___ for me?"
126 Indy car sponsor
127 Tending to shrink?
128 Rice field
129 Gaze longingly at

DOWN

1 A
2 Something to grind
3 **Dam adjunct**
4 Play section
5 Old letter that *w* replaced
6 "___ a fact!"
7 Diamond robberies?
8 Dog from hell?
9 Sun. talk
10 Helical blueprint
11 Beef thief
12 Equal to the task
13 Horse or Plymouth
14 My ___, Vietnam
15 Aluminum giant
17 Soft colors
19 Top number?
20 Slick-road hazard
22 Cousin of 10 Down
24 Roundabout
29 Reader's card
30 "First lady of the theater"
31 Verne character
32 "___ of thousands"
33 Egg carton word
34 Animal lovers' org.
37 ___ out (canceled)
38 Time for St. Agnes
39 *The Invisible Man* star
41 Foundation
42 Deli sandwiches
43 Disdains
45 Gold Coast, today
46 Pub. defenders
47 Extreme reaction
49 Dorothy's guardian
51 A Cape
54 In Tours, yours truly
56 Sneaky or sleazy type
59 Ex of Artie and Frank
61 Witnessed
62 Jong and Kane
64 Sun Devils' school
66 Place down solidly
67 Scoundrel
68 On the money
70 Eastern leader
71 O'clock or so
72 African language
74 Frankfurter or the Cat
77 Swedish auto
79 Blender setting
81 Essay writing, e.g.
83 Played a band instrument
85 **Widening, as pupils**
86 Scripture section
87 Jet black
89 Slinky killer
91 Subway ancestors
92 United group
94 Charity event
96 Doctor, as a photo
99 Shaft of a feather
100 Covered
101 Add on
103 Type of reaction
104 Part of BART
105 Delineates
108 *Falstaff* or *Faust*
109 Actress Scala
110 Pitcher's ERA, e.g.
112 Complain
113 The eighth mo., once
117 Androgynous character on *Saturday Night Live*
118 Man of art
119 Skip stones across water
120 Humorist Blount Jr.
121 Zip
122 Former phone co.

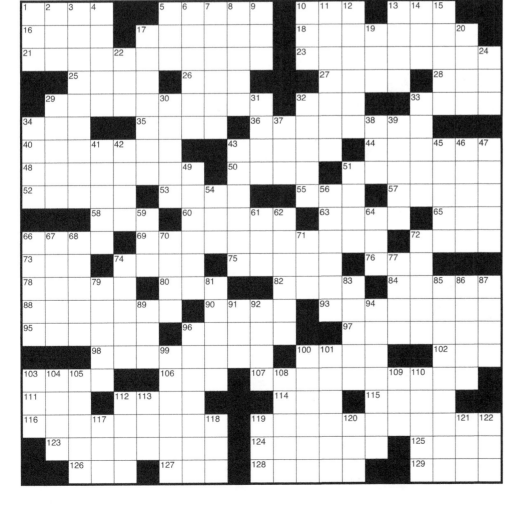

ACROSS

1 Singer of literature
6 Slain brother of Charles Evers
12 Rough-shaping tool
15 The end, to Truffaut
18 When taxpayers get a break
20 Carry to excess
21 *Calvin & Hobbes* bully
22 Lizzie's "whacks" applicator
23 Late-night intro, once
26 Superior and Supreme: abbr.
27 Chinese concept
28 *The Joy Luck Club* author
29 R. Murrow or G. Robinson
30 Nondiscriminatory
32 Where Hercules slew a lion
34 Carbon, oxygen, etc.
37 Wine, with "the"
38 Western exit line
44 Freed from Cleveland
45 "Life ___" (or vice versa)
46 Tarzan's kid
47 Mr. Chaney
48 Mercury and Saturn
50 Cleanse anew
52 Funnyman's signature line
58 Hamilton's bill
59 Bridal path
61 Flavoring plant
62 Brief subject?

63 1920s gangster "Mad Dog"
65 Give consent
69 Vocalist Frankie
71 1960s snack slogan
77 *Enterprise* officer
78 Durocher nickname
79 Geraldine's mom
80 Pick: abbr.
81 Willing
84 Company based in Hartford
86 Was ahead of
89 Another late-night intro
94 Gorgeous, in a way
97 Scandinavian capital
98 Prefix meaning "shoulder"
99 *Red River* actress
101 Bert's muppet mate
102 Swimmer with a big mouth?
105 Another funnyman's signature line
109 Clowning
111 "___ Ike"
112 Latin base meaning "holy"
113 Under state?
116 Greek letter
118 Kin of "yecch"
119 Poisonous snake
122 Close-encounter reaction
123 Apt closer to this puzzle
128 Gym-floor buffer

129 Low digit?
130 Fax over
131 Gobs and scads
132 Ocean OK
133 Withdrawal mach.
134 Map blowups, sometimes
135 Schedule again

DOWN

1 "The wolf ___ the door"
2 Will be, in a song
3 "As if that weren't enough ..."
4 Citrus drink
5 Races
6 Holstein hello
7 Carouser's cry, in old Greece
8 East Indian cedar
9 Shoot up
10 Brouhaha
11 Pal of Pooh
12 To ___ (unanimously)
13 Knucklehead
14 Woody's "chameleon"
15 Salon offering
16 Mexico vacation spot
17 Ford aide who hosted *Saturday Night Live*
19 Orange Bowl city
24 Steak wt., perhaps

25 ___ bone to pick
31 Generals, generally
32 Half of a sleuthing duo
33 Acknowledges
35 Old words of anguish
36 Tailless cat
38 "Sugar Lips" trumpeter
39 Fortuneteller's words
40 Ennui evidence
41 Maybelline target
42 Chills
43 Part of BYOB
49 City of great pubs
51 Gag answer to "How many people work in your office?"
53 Milk, in Mazatlán
54 Chastity's mom
55 Qualified: abbr.
56 Bison feature
57 Woolly belles
60 "Okay, ___ bite"
63 "Scoundrel," minus six letters
64 "Rock ___" (hymn)
66 Either Ripken
67 Bottled water from France
68 Banks (on)
70 Lord Byron's daughter
71 Be in a hurry
72 Korea's Syngman
73 Do a judge's job
74 Are, to André
75 First name of 17 Down
76 Trucker's life, with "the"
82 Alice's balladeer
83 Cat's cry
85 Newcomers
86 Star "discovered at Schwab's" (but not really)
87 Arab VIP
88 Not natural, in a way
90 Microscope-slide dye
91 Dewlap relative
92 It means "all"
93 Arcing overhead throw, in basketball
95 Try to grab
96 Part of Q.E.D.
100 Trailer-rental co.
102 Grand ___ Island
103 Be that as it may
104 Florida city, for short
106 Bone-breaking tradition
107 Exam taker
108 Part of WASP
110 Terra ___
114 Useless from too much use
115 Gossip unit
117 "That ___ fair!"
119 "___ well that ends..."
120 With "Ball," a classic arcade game
121 Library attention-getter
124 Next after bi
125 Feathered layer
126 Magazines, mostly
127 Certain poem

ACROSS

1 Hits a high, catchable fly
9 Use the hold
13 Houston of Texas
16 Nth degree, nowadays
19 Parthian shot
20 *Damn Yankees* character
21 "___ takers?"
22 Steve's co-star in *The Getaway*
23 Restaurant order
25 Actor Eric of *49th Parallel*
27 Am or ox ending
28 Inexperienced chalk user's sound
29 Restaurant order
31 Emulate Edward Scissorhands
34 Restaurant order, with 36 Across
36 See 34 Across
39 Exclude
40 Province opposite Mich.
41 Make an impression
43 It means "1,000,000,000th"
44 It means "5"
49 Settle down
51 Caught
53 Eyelash
54 Overwhelm
55 Theater line?
56 A sport of kings
58 See 9 Across
60 Restaurant order
63 Region
65 Den clamor
66 Restaurant order
74 Acolyte's place
79 Rating scale, often
80 Greek letters
81 Sharpened
83 Capital W of Montreal
84 Tummy tighteners
87 Beyond PG-13
88 Webster's namesakes
89 Story line
91 Second-largest asteroid
93 Pastoral plaint
94 Like boxers before a bout
96 Restaurant order
98 Restaurant order
104 Things you do
105 Restaurant order
106 Common French verb
107 Liked lots
109 "... sitting ___, K-I-S-S-I-N-G"
110 Restaurant order
116 D.C. employee
117 Polish name ending
118 Meeting place?
119 Refinement
120 Put it to
121 Unsurpassed ending
122 Tyco products
123 Cold War warming trends

DOWN

1 Sing Sing, e.g.
2 Losing line of tic-tac-toe
3 Movie, in *Variety*
4 Mark of rank
5 "Where Is the Life That Late ___?"
6 It goes out twice a day
7 It means "1"
8 Short-lived 1970s craze
9 It shares a key with ?
10 Apathetic
11 Yesterday's news
12 Lukewarm review
13 1972 Winter Olympics city
14 Celebes oxen
15 "Gold and frankincense and ___"
16 1950s First Lady
17 Young and Hale
18 Crosswalk, on a sign
24 Milk protein
26 Ref's ruling
30 ___ even keel
31 The hoity-toity, to the hoi polloi
32 Reason for silent teletypes
33 "___ All There Is?"
34 Diarist Anaïs
35 Extends a subscription
37 Invite inserts
38 Compete
42 Voice-over: abbr.
44 Scottish ancestor
45 The Morlocks ate them
46 Fashion's Cerruti
47 Become rancid
48 Carter and Grant
50 M.D.'s org.
52 Wade foe, once
53 Barton or Bow
56 Calaveras competitor
57 She was Sarah in *The Bible* (1966)
59 "___ luego"
60 Nuremberg negative
61 Quaker tidbit
62 East end?
64 Hwy.
66 Hour of reckoning for Will Kane (Gary Cooper)
67 Word after glom or latch
68 ___ spell (get right comfy)
69 Home of Bryce Canyon
70 Perlman purchases
71 Joins forces
72 Famous boy king
73 "The jig ___!"
75 Tibet's capital
76 Little one
77 Antonym of "robust"
78 Tiny warrior
82 Goes numbingly slow
84 Most like a judge, perhaps
85 Can and cup place
86 Having large, dark peepers
87 Kin of "Fight fiehcely, Hahvahd"
89 Skeptic's challenge
90 Pierced place
92 Leary tried it
95 Platter spinner
97 Bag lady's mate?
98 Ebbs
99 1938 film, ___ at Oxford
100 End of a believer
101 Laconic
102 Arduous journeys
103 Big Bang material?
105 Birthplace of Galileo
107 "I Remember It Well," e.g.
108 It may be uncontrollable
111 Modernist's prefix
112 The last thing a bull may hear
113 Tolkien being, Treebeard the ___
114 Part of a "dead man's hand"
115 Guitar pioneer Paul

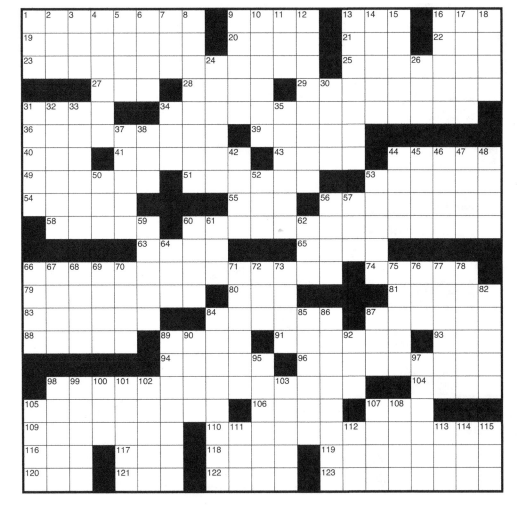

...Beware of "accident"-al tourists

ACROSS

1 Greedy
8 High-potassium fruit
14 Bat, for one
20 Siren
21 Words rarely heard down at police headquarters
22 "___ inside me said ..."
23 Not yet signed, to *Variety*
24 _____ + O
26 Playing surface No. 1
27 Real name of Roy Rogers, Leonard ___
28 Cash back?
29 Jazz writer Hentoff
30 True statement
31 Arizona Indian
33 Play the dating game
36 Something to do on Tuesday
37 Beatle's wife
38 CO + _____
42 Pledge of Allegiance wds.
43 Monumental
44 Cleveland deejay who popularized the term "rock 'n' roll"
45 Taping abbr.
46 Jaguar scar
47 South Carolina river
48 Delibes opera
52 Topical comic
54 Manorial menial
56 Like George's view of the future
58 Oy follower
60 Peace in the Middle East?
64 D.C. denizen
65 Cpl., for one
66 Puts up with
69 Name of San Francisco's famous 101 Across (and the basis of this puzzle)
72 Gets stuck
74 Makin' bacon place
75 Xylem and phloem fluid
77 Visas and passports
79 Bankroll
80 Bit of symbolic writing
84 OSU foe
86 Recovery ctr.
89 It's "human"
90 Concert hall key?
94 Zest, for example
96 Impair
97 Caltech, for one
99 Bond villain
100 Partner of "the same"
101 See 69 Across
104 Drug banner: abbr.
105 Cartoonist Addams, in his signatures
106 Like krypton or xenon
107 *Day of the Locust* climax
108 Luchino's *Death in Venice* star
109 Stagnant situation
110 Rained out: abbr.
111 Brilliant stroke
113 Satellite of Saturn
114 _____
119 "I Love ___"
121 Kin of "allow me"
122 The Peabody and others
123 Wrapped cheese slices
124 Hollywood boulevard
125 Most recent
126 ___ for (is desirous of)

DOWN

1 Sportswear, once
2 Ithaca's waters
3 _____ + I
4 Jean of the Theatre of the Absurd
5 Actress Chase
6 "What'd I tell ya?"
7 Played a child's game
8 Book opening?
9 Call it ___
10 Prime time time
11 Do a tax return chore
12 Nonexistent
13 Had some grub or some grubs
14 ___ grade (measured up)
15 State unequivocally
16 Where Fez is: abbr.
17 Filet ___
18 Having a sharp point
19 Philippine island
25 They work on planes
27 Ghostly
31 Revs up the P.R. machine
32 Speaks thoughtfully
33 *The Nanny* first name
34 Slow, to Simon Rattle
35 Draw a conclusion
36 *Palimpsest* author
38 *Hazel* creator Key
39 Music notes
40 Where Naples is: abbr.
41 "What have we here?"
49 _____ + Y
50 Spray weapon
51 Slaughter of baseball
53 Had the fewest strokes
55 Andy Capp's better half
57 Ambusher of the deep
59 Basic choice
61 Roadie's armful
62 Bar grp.
63 Driver's aid
66 M.D.'s 2 o'clock, e.g.
67 *Charles in Charge* star
68 Union with an acting head?
70 See 64 Across
71 Leaky faucet sound
73 Morse morsel
76 Indulges in a fantasy
78 Headphone effect
81 The Stooges and others
82 Organic compound
83 Alma ___
85 Precept
87 Alexandra Zuck, in films
88 Triple Crown leg
91 Simply
92 Melvin who could hit
93 Thing, in law
95 Place to sell cars
98 Forgets the whole thing
101 Burnett-Arkin film, ___ *and the Philly Flash*
102 Furniture palm
103 Most constant
105 Hardly Mr. Sensitive
108 Funeral hymn
110 Kilauea's fire goddess
111 Basic, as beliefs
112 Ransom of cars
113 Beach browns
115 Capt. Flint's creator
116 50 Down container
117 Feeling to be struck with
118 Like sashimi
119 Furnace coating
120 Actress Zadora

ACROSS

1 Canoe-bark tree
6 Tyke's tender
10 Parts of a flight
15 Live in sewers, for example?
19 Palmer, to pals
20 Biggest dessert at the Rodent Diner?
22 The ___ Carta
23 Related
24 Guinea pig tender
25 Dry, cold wind of France and Switzerland
27 Docking place
28 "Well, whattaya know!"
29 Jessye Norman selection
32 Pitcairn, for one: abbr.
34 Yasir, that's his baby: abbr.
36 SSW U-turn
37 New pet rodent?
42 Hidden hikers
44 Popular beverage at the Rodent Diner?
45 ___-schmancy
46 Dance great Alicia
48 Soldier adjective
49 Latin word on a bill
51 Pisa's river
52 *Au* alternative
53 Top bond rating
54 Shampoo brand
55 Rich rodents' home?

61 Tony Randall film, *7 Faces of Dr.* ___
63 "Doo-dah" lead-in
64 Munchkin kin
65 Locate
67 Literary monogram
69 "___ man answers ..."
72 Nile ophidian
74 Rodent's favorite snack?
79 Dixon's colleague
81 Enjoy empanadas, e.g.
83 Capybara's home in the city
84 Puts the cuffs on
85 Handle shape, in space
86 Dental degree
87 Greek sun god
91 Musical Joplin
92 With 97 Across, a line from a rodent fairy tale?
95 Fries lightly
97 See 92 Across
99 Sapporo sash
100 Investment in the future?
101 Fine all around
102 Church section
103 Opp. of 8 Down
106 Exam adjective
108 Name-change nation
110 Start of the second half of the 6th century
112 Walt Kelly character
113 Radiated happiness

115 Most popular dessert at the Rodent Diner?
121 "And it won't cost you ___"
122 Rodent tycoon?
123 Hollywood Hopper
124 "___ old pappy used to say ..."
125 Fish sandwiches

DOWN

1 Bingo call
2 Her, to Hesse
3 Bakker was one: abbr.
4 Magnon intro
5 Honey-sesame seed candy
6 Helens intro
7 Asian gazelle (or a topless Hawaiian island?)
8 Musical abbr.
9 Cole Porter show, *Red, Hot,* ___
10 *Casablanca* pianist
11 Lobster catcher
12 Masterminded
13 Evergreen "leaf"
14 Browned quickly, as tuna
15 Edward K. Ellington
16 Mayberry moppet
17 Prop for 19 Across
18 Carefree, to Camille
20 Old bed condition

21 Extra-noteworthy
26 "Bennie and the Jets" singer
29 16 Down's pop
30 Pooh pal
31 "___ in the wrist"
32 Little homewreckers
33 London restaurant hub
35 Fighting sound effect on TV's *Batman*
37 Cozy recess
38 Mind's I
39 Secretariat rider Turcotte
40 Young lady of Sp.
41 1973 Orson Welles film about frauds, ___ *Fake*
42 Soft or hard products
43 Freud's daughter
45 Beatles adjective
47 Puts
50 Bullshout
52 Canine comments
53 Piedmont town
54 Game played with mallets
56 Verve
57 Sword handle
58 Ore ending
59 Abner's pal, on radio
60 Escape route?
62 Exxon rival
66 Mr. Ferrari
68 "Moonlight," for one
69 "___ little confused ..."
70 *Funny Girl* subject
71 Press adjective
73 Boringly explanatory
75 Loose talk
76 Welles role
77 Nile avian
78 Mountain road shape
80 President's promise
82 Like a grate
86 Units of force, in physics
87 Crackers brand
88 Composer Satie
89 He was the Wolfman
90 Popular business mag
91 Styne at the Steinway
93 Lobster catcher?
94 See 117 Down
96 Tipper's guy and others
97 The elusive spondulix
98 Ashbury crosser
103 Rodentlike insectivore
104 Too much sun or worry, for example
105 Gleason's bartender
107 Ingrid Bergman's character in *Casablanca*, Ilsa ___
109 "Gotcha!"
110 Say (it) isn't so
111 Trip "vehicle" of the 1960s
112 Worst
114 Educ. liaison
116 Shatner and Shak.
117 With 94 Down, play on which *Cabaret* is based
118 ___ de Cologne
119 He lost to JFK
120 Jamboree org.

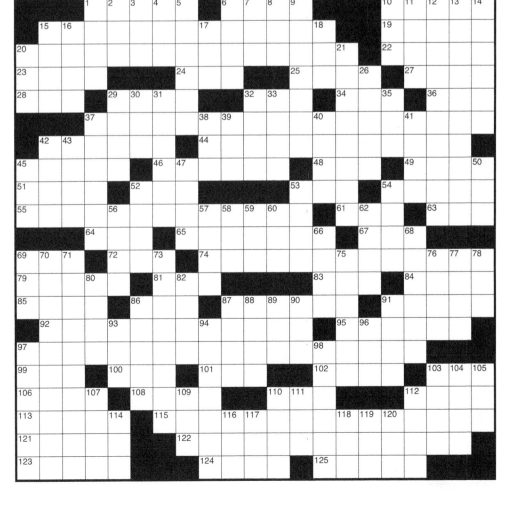

ACROSS

1 Oaxacan OK
8 ___ down (inverted)
14 Penne et al.
19 Dye category
20 Crazy ___
21 The gift of acting?
22 Where mollusk grievances are settled?
24 One of a quotable 150
25 Big rig
26 Adjust, Tim Allen-style
27 Simone's sea
29 Nevada city
30 Lou Grant's "Happy Homemaker," ___ Nivens
32 1989 film, ___-Devil
34 Horse tender at an inn
36 Joan, to John Cusack
39 Clinic VIPs
40 Have some brewskis at a mollusk bar?
44 "Kid" of jazz fame
45 Taken, as a seat on Mollusk Airways?
48 Other, to Orozco
49 Let out ___ (show shock)
51 Examiner exec
52 1934 song, "The Sweetest Music This Side ___"
55 Of an insect stage
58 3-D circles
59 Cold, in Colombia
60 It means "five"
62 "Passenger loading," e.g.
63 "All is calm, all ___"
67 Warning shout when slop is thrown out a window
69 With 109 Across, from a plane
72 Fashion item for today's busy mollusk?
75 It's a gas: abbr.
76 Desecrated
78 "In ___ purple-black ..." (G.K. Chesterton)
80 A Chekhov sister
81 Conductor Seiji
84 Currier & ___
85 Mus. work
89 John of tractordom
91 Some makeup
93 Jason's quest
95 Siren sound, in the comics
97 Reddish brown
98 Last stop for downtrodden mollusks?
100 Rukeyser's old series: abbr.
102 Toast heard at a kosher mollusk wedding?
105 Diminutive suffix
106 Pink Scrabble square: abbr.
107 Prepare leftovers
109 See 69 Across
110 Ferdinand wed her
113 Tees off
114 Calendar abbr.
116 Ex-Senator Paul from Nevada
118 Use UPS
122 Like a delta's bottom
124 Mollusk's favorite sci-fi series?
128 Word with care or ticket
129 Stop sign plus one?
130 Vast holdings
131 Fizz fruits
132 Wait ___
133 Pepe Le Pew's problem?

DOWN

1 Lip
2 "I didn't know I had it ___"
3 Anna's second home
4 New York island
5 Zip, nada, goose egg
6 In installments
7 Free, as a hand brake
8 Most of Asia, once: abbr.
9 Wait for baby?
10 ___-mo (replay speed, for short)
11 Red marker
12 Roof window
13 Heraldry term
14 Ricky's term for Ozzie
15 Personal plus
16 Sampling of mollusk opinion?
17 Loquacious one
18 Military building
20 ___ acids
23 Oat bristle
28 Director Nicolas
31 Authorities on the field
32 Helmet adjunct
33 Ho's predecessor?
35 Trade
36 London area
37 Cold storage
38 Gladiator wound
41 Rum drinker's refrain
42 Sault ___ Marie
43 Rear-end features of some birds and fish
46 Bears, in Italy
47 Rock Hudson co-star, often
50 Actress Parker
53 Kadota fruit
54 Participants
56 Soon, once
57 Actor Carroll
59 Fridge parts
61 Guitarist Guthrie
64 Refreshing spot
65 Czech Republic city
66 Explosive
68 Brit. award
69 Like two peas in ___
70 Perry's creator
71 Mollusk signoff?
73 Japanese religion
74 Actress Campbell of Party of Five
77 Klinger portrayer
79 Garrulous equine
82 "If I ___ Rich Man"
83 ___ in the conversation
86 Buffalo bunch
87 "Don't have ___, man!" (Bart Simpson)
88 Sermon seating
90 Ms. Bombeck
92 Follower's ending
93 40 hours a week
94 Prevaricated
96 Places people get stuck
99 Put down, as a riot
100 Watch spots
101 Soap, for example
103 Draw off
104 Female fox
108 Ms. Lauder
111 Scratch, for example
112 Shivering dish
115 Sicilian spewer
116 Olympic sled
117 Stub ___
119 Ici, in Indiana
120 Interstate across the southern U.S.
121 Sibilant attention-getter
123 Info on wine bottles: abbr.
125 Last page
126 Americas alliance: abbr.
127 Base watchdogs, familiarly

ACROSS

1 Sitting ___ stoplight
4 "Last of his tribe" Indian of California
8 Fuss
11 Ruhr city
16 Conspicuousness symbol
19 Knighting words, "___ thee"
21 Baryshnikov's birthplace
23 **Humpty Dumpty's 911 call?**
26 Poky tree dwellers
27 Boob
28 They might be full of beans
29 Gymnast's pointer?
30 **Infrequent flyer's worry?**
36 Stable females
39 Samantha's mom
40 Critical
41 Imitator
42 Beatty or Buntline
43 Norm of golf
46 Texturally rough
50 Local law: abbr.
51 **Transplant outcome?**
56 **Drastic cure for an acid stomach?**
58 Period
59 Air safety org.
60 Lobster catcher?
61 ___ de la Cité
62 Actor Joslyn
64 Junior on the journal
66 Nitti's pistols
67 **With 80 Across, *Friday the 13th, Part 10*?**
72 Speakeasy passphrase, "Joe ___ me"
73 ___ large extent
74 They get walked on
75 Pear-shaped fruit
76 Drink "for two"
77 Wallower's home
79 Deck total, to a Roman
80 **See 67 Across**
83 **Lonely film fan's wish?**
89 *Sun-Times* city, familiarly
91 Moses watched this part
92 Friend of *la famille*
93 Common verb
94 Church closing?
95 Appease totally
97 Schindler and Werner
101 Football fan's quaffs
102 **With 115 Across, "Weird Al" Yankovic's boast?**
108 ___ Na Na
109 Sports figure?
110 It did a Prizm make
111 Baker and Bryant
115 **See 102 Across**
121 Sound car investment?
122 *Peter Pan* pooch
123 Wink
124 Good ___ (cured)
125 Noggin bob
126 Fifth of five, e.g.
127 Mr. Caesar

DOWN

1 Indiana Jones hates them
2 Hammer or sickle
3 Group W bench sitter, in a 1960s song and movie
4 Makes one scratch
5 Tom Jones hit, "___ Lady"
6 " 'Scuse me?"
7 George Harrison book, ___ *Mine*
8 Have one's sights set on
9 Pres. from Denison, Tex.
10 Prophetic board
11 Stretchy, to Maria
12 Abe Vigoda's *Godfather* role, ___ Tessio
13 Letters on a Cardinal's cap
14 Madonna role
15 Sheer fabric
17 One or the other
18 Like Bjorn's locks
20 Key with five sharps: abbr.
22 *The African Queen* scriptwriter
24 Half a Samoan city
25 J. ___ Muggs (Garroway's *Today* show chimp)
31 Turns sharply
32 May auto race
33 Vintage valley
34 Person with class?
35 True, to a Scot
36 Peking kingpin, once
37 Fool's day: abbr.
38 Black 7 topper, in solitaire
42 "Just say what you want"
44 Cat fancier from Melmac
45 Fails a stoic's test
47 Moroccan capital
48 Snuffy or Loweezy
49 Goes from better to worse
51 To spice, as cider
52 Position of control
53 Where Van Gogh painted *Sunflowers*
54 " ... in the pot, nine ___"
55 France, once
57 Pinball penalty
62 Hercule's creator
63 "The truth"
65 Three-___ card
66 Jazz jobs
67 Actor Brasselle
68 Grant-___ (scholarship)
69 Like a snoop
70 Irish nationalist org., Sinn ___
71 Smart-mouthed
72 Confinement
78 Thanksgiving sweet
80 Author Fannie
81 Zenith
82 "That was close!"
84 Bone prefix
85 Very legible
86 Midnight movie
87 *"Vaya Con ___"*
88 Husk-y bunch
90 Allstate's bus.
94 She expresses herself easel-ly
96 Cigar's end
98 "I'm ___ you could make it!"
99 Dress length
100 "___ of grass-green silk she wore" (Tennyson)
101 Masked marauder
102 Dogmatic topics
103 "Sheesh! ___ grouch!"
104 Makes a pile in autumn
105 Pvt. Benjamin's portrayer
106 Allen or Frome
107 Discontinues
112 Ramon's relatives
113 Curtain raiser
114 Agenda, briefly
116 No way to address Hemingway?
117 Some people drive off it
118 *Two Virgins* album poser
119 Cruet contents
120 Elvis's record label

ACROSS

1 One who makes and sells fashionable dresses and hats for women
8 Irritable
19 From within, in Latin
20 Singer who survived the 1906 San Francisco quake
21 Gluey
22 Short on schooling
23 Roman emperor who saw a flaming cross in the sky
25 Double-curve shapes
26 Reenacts
28 No smoking in the office, for example
29 Manx thanks
32 Sea swallows
33 Dorm sound
34 Claimed, in a way
39 Followers of *The King*
40 Director's cut?
41 Ornamental flower stand
42 Symbol of redness
43 Railroad that Jay Gould and Cornelius Vanderbilt fought over
44 Group that slides stones on ice at the Olympics
45 Sharpened, as a razor

47 Ken's friend
48 Inasmuch as
49 *Hiver* opposite
50 Wine region
52 The Big Easy, in shorthand
53 Error
57 Court cutups
58 *A Walk on the Wild Side* author Nelson
60 Barometer unit
61 Criticizing as worthless
63 Medical grp.
64 Summer ermine
66 Signs up for
67 Fabric store bargains
72 Like card tables
74 Simple
75 Setting of Martin Scorsese's *After Hours*
76 Misjudges, in a way
77 No basis for discrimination
78 Vincent's brother
79 Chuck Yeager, e.g.
80 Washing-up pot
81 Making crosswords, for one
82 Maturing agent
83 Knight's weapon
84 Supports a kid?
85 17-syllable poem

89 Appellation in Handel's *Messiah*
91 Announcer's signoff
95 Shoe parts
98 Deejay employer
99 Appear, to Shakespeare
100 Star of *Show Boat* on stage and screen
101 Certifies

DOWN

1 Dallas player, for short
2 Part of Alec Guinness's name in *Star Wars*
3 Rummy player, often
4 Under an alias
5 Slingshot missiles
6 Tie (up)
7 From Eden to Nod
8 Robert Frost poem, *Fire ___*
9 The Council of ___
10 To laugh, to Lalo
11 Bandage maker
12 Pride of Mr. Universe
13 Hosp. unit
14 Cousins of ant lions
15 Levin et al.
16 Ending for black, brown, or burn

17 Beneficiary of a lawsuit, at times
18 Plants grass
20 Whole
22 Erased
24 Vergil verse
26 Shots (at)
27 Principle
29 TV host Perkins and ex-White House aide Fitzwater
30 Whirled, as water
31 Frigg's hubby
33 Mountainside debris
34 *The Wizard of Oz* lyricist
35 Heavily satirical
36 "And he was never ___ heard from again"
37 Prophet at Delphi
38 ___ lion, beast slain by Hercules
40 Music for 7
41 Actor Curt
44 Radial, e.g.
46 *Un ___* (a little)
47 32-quart units
50 Recommended choice
51 Talk loudly
53 Lopped lousily
54 Chant
55 Viragoes
56 Alpine home
57 Broom room bigwig
59 Boris contemporary
62 Kind of real estate deal, for example
63 Wading bird
65 Waterproof cover
67 Disaster aid
68 1992 GOP convention site
69 Credit union promise
70 Larceny
71 Marks with chimney dirt
73 Smug one
74 Russia or Idaho city
77 Straight talk
80 Unfruitful
81 Waist nipper
83 Woman of the Doones
84 With 90 Down, *A Different World* actress
85 Nervous moment of silence
86 A bettor opening
87 Foreign-wd. type
88 Golfer Tom
89 Certain bass note
90 See 84 Down
92 The pauper, not the prince
93 "Give Peace A Chance" video participant
94 *Casablanca*'s country: abbr.
96 Werner Erhard's self-awareness program of the 1970s
97 Peter, Paul, and Mary: abbr.

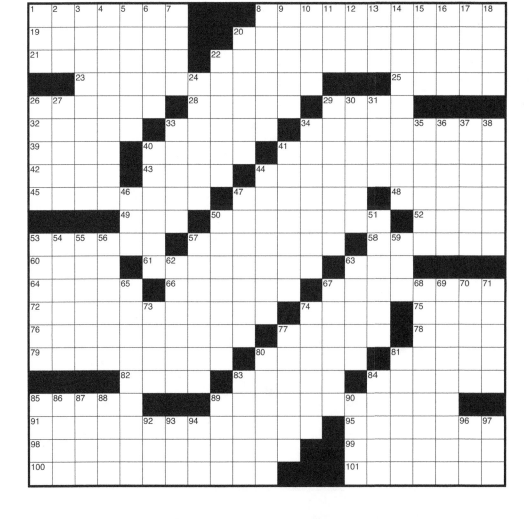

Once Upon an Island

...Might as well give up—you're surrounded

ACROSS

1 Let bygones be bygones
7 Angry moms' grp.
11 Jolt with volts
14 Guy in the Garden
18 Cuban choreographer
19 Actress Braga
20 Chicken preceder
21 Star-search trio
22 Forum footwear
23 Island query to a slowpoke?
26 Addn. result
27 Gets rid of messages
29 Neufchâtel negative
30 Out of the sack
31 Simple, in island lingo?
34 *Ragtime* penner's inits.
36 Artifact hunt
38 Carbo concluder
39 Humiliate
40 Didn't last long on the islands?
43 " ... cup ___ over"
46 One up?
48 Aero or para finisher
49 Arden or Taylor: abbr.
50 "Up 'n' ___!"
52 Make perfectly clear
54 Woodwinds
58 Caesar's comment after his island vacation?
62 Moderate, to Mozart
64 *"Ich ___ ein Berliner"*
65 Lower-class, in Britain
66 Where Bend is: abbr.
67 Siamese sound
68 Solving crosswords on an island?
74 Sty guy
75 League plant
76 Something to stick in your shoe
77 Softball, camping, etc.: abbr.
78 Ulna
80 Popular singer on the island?
85 Sherpa's home
86 TV spy whose name was created by Ian Fleming
89 "___ long way down"
90 Easy victory
91 Wheat alternative
93 French dances
95 "Am-scray!"
98 "Am-scray!" on the island?
101 Athenian statesman
102 Cruise (about)
103 *Frontline* network
104 Sequel to *She*?
105 Feature of Elmer Fudd's island home?
109 Computer game name
111 Point to, as the piccolos
113 Finally

115 Specialty of 101 Across
116 Puzzlemaker's thought as island solvers chase him?
119 Gauguin was here
122 First name in whodunits
123 Coin-___
124 Think alike
125 Oozes
126 Radiator sound
127 According to
128 Hoses (down)
129 Hook up to a polygraph again

DOWN

1 Tall, pastoral nomads of Africa
2 Gentle as ___
3 "___ know you?"
4 Final analysis
5 Mex.-door neighbor?
6 Aromatic animal
7 Antlered animal
8 James II's daughter
9 Anatomize
10 Doo follower
11 Number of times Garbo was married
12 To-do list
13 Club owner's club?
14 Golfer Alcott and an Alcott character
15 Scopes trial city
16 Stereotyper of seniors
17 A pope's hat, to A. Pope
19 Get dry, dog style
24 Still its original color
25 Herb Woodley's neighbor
28 Phylicia or Ahmad
32 Former soap opera set on an island?
33 Oft-quoted prez
35 "Where Is the Life That ___ Led?"
37 Elected ones
41 Modern med. diagnostic technique
42 Popular island dish?
43 Give a lot of gas?
44 Diminutive suffix
45 Noted diarist
46 Make muddled
47 Type of acid
51 Like the sound of a cheap toy horn
53 The O'Hara estate
55 Neither aye nor eye has this
56 Ian Fleming attended it
57 Isaac Singer made it easier to do this
59 Actor Tayback
60 Finish, as a sketch
61 Coup group
63 Indian jacket
66 Doesn't resist
68 Had on
69 Wheelchair access
70 Composer Charles
71 Pulitzer-winning Pyle
72 Factions of faith
73 Type of sleep
74 Prohibition
79 Swimming-pool size
80 "Really?!"
81 Cabbages and kings?
82 Overly
83 Living qtrs.
84 Copy
87 More than one 20 Across
88 Agitated state
92 Lessen
94 McNamara's middle name
96 1969 pop hit, "Take ___, Maria"
97 Lawn order
98 Florida collegians
99 Mo and Stew of Arizona
100 Prisoner's preoccupation
101 Tai ties one on
102 I'll play these
105 Turns on a pivot
106 Use airflow for lift
107 Loathes
108 New wrinkle
110 Regrets
112 Georgia's home, formerly: abbr.
114 Civil wrong
117 Beat pounder
118 Detroit org.
120 Tool for Bunyan
121 Hiking word

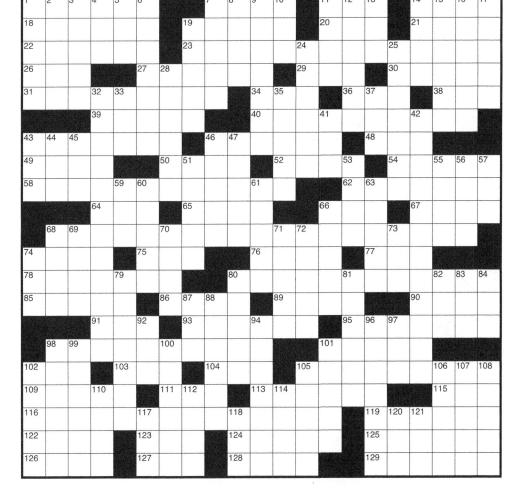

ACROSS

1 Kuwaiti kingpins
6 Deep opera voices
11 Puberty problem
15 2 on the phone
18 Ledger entry
19 Backyard soak
20 Bok ___
21 His counterpart
22 Night reminder to a lamb?
25 First name in interchangeable parts
26 Foot division
27 Forgotten in the rain
28 Architect Saarinen
29 Thomas of Wendy's
30 Slangy nose
32 Start of a lamb's favorite play?
35 Candice's dad
38 Voice of Daffy
39 Bradstreet's buddy
40 Follow like sheep
43 Nicholas Gage book
46 El ___ (slangy cigar)
49 End of the title at 32 Across
53 Subject for Grisham
54 Book about lamb-style Little League?
57 It's after boo or before boy
58 Berkelium or californium
60 TV player
61 Gala get-together
62 Cole Porter's Indiana birthplace
63 The Audubon, e.g.: abbr.
64 Joey's "steps"
66 Shad delicacy
67 Unit next to the mgr.'s, perhaps
68 Closing remark to a lamb encounter group?
74 Bug spray brand
75 Sphere
76 Josh
77 Broke bread
78 Right
79 Proclamation
81 Most intense: abbr.
82 A page from antiquity?
86 ___-disant (so-called)
87 Lamb's favorite class?
90 1953 fantasy, *The 5,000 Fingers of ___*
91 Owner's document
93 Category of instrument
94 Simple soup
95 Letters to Manhattan?
96 "Here ___!"
98 Contraction of the season
100 Tiny Tom
102 What a lamb might have when he grows up?
109 More well-heeled
113 He's *Incredible*
114 Many miles away
115 Block buster?
118 "Strange Magic" grp.
119 A kiss between hugs?
120 Lamb in the penthouse?
123 Convertible's roof
124 ___ instant
125 Brosnan role
126 Clinton colleague Shalala
127 Metal container?
128 Sites of winding rds.
129 Basket fiber
130 Balboa named one

DOWN

1 Gloria's mom
2 Conformist's motto
3 Gabler's creator
4 Grave letters
5 Looked into space?
6 Pay-per-view event
7 Courtyards
8 Off. employee
9 With mixed veggies, in Chinese cuisine
10 "When Will ___ Loved"
11 Behaved
12 Tweet substitute?
13 "I'm in ___ for your games"
14 Once-over
15 Winning
16 Author Plain
17 Did a sad thing
19 Lofty areas: abbr.
23 Big-time operator?
24 ___ the bottom of the deck
29 Early Bond foe
31 Combination alternative
33 *Jurassic Park* star
34 Unseat
36 *Beaucoup*, over here
37 M.L.K. Jr., for one
40 Shout that's 118 Across backwards
41 Dance, in France
42 Lamb's mom's favorite expression?
44 Not once
45 "The die ___"
47 Cardin or Curie
48 "... ___ thought"
50 Lamb's favorite game show?
51 Out line of a heart?
52 Uncertainty
54 "Shucks"
55 Popular movie theater name
56 British gun
59 Sophia's world
62 *Cry-Baby* co-star Hearst
64 Roundish, as some leaves
65 Navy underwater project of the 1960s
68 Word in bank names
69 SE Asian capital
70 Where couch potatoes are planted
71 Tuck, for one
72 ___ *Is Born*
73 Spaces
80 Start of a Henry James title
82 Rind lining
83 "Silent as ___" (Charlotte Brontë)
84 Grecian collectible
85 Chester White's home
87 Tyrannosaurus Rex's diet
88 Have a typo personality?
89 Little cutie
92 Connect
95 Chancellor's channel
97 Graham Greene's *Travels with ___*
99 Periods of work
101 Nanki-Poo's pop (with "the")
102 Picture ID
103 Temple of Amon site
104 Run off to tie the knot
105 "What manner ___ is this?"
106 Principal water pipes
107 Eightsome
108 Stairway post
110 German poet and satirist, 1797-1856
111 1956 Ingrid Bergman film, ___ *and Her Men*
112 Martin partner, once
116 Carpet feature
117 127 Across ending
120 Tire mount
121 "___ said before ..."
122 Singing: abbr.

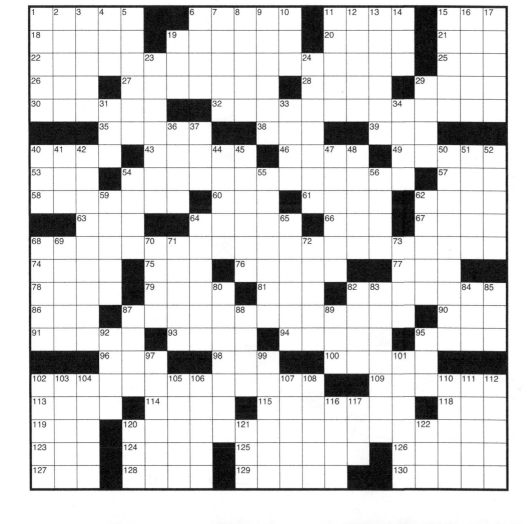

ACROSS

1 "___ in 'apple'"
4 *La Prensa* article?
7 Carry
11 Antique
16 ... a *Hart to Hart* star acting a little wooden?
19 Delphi know-it-all
21 ... a *Today* show host in a fowl mood?
22 Pitching style
24 Result of a sap judgment
25 Relation
26 Grammarian's gripes, perhaps
28 Perfect square
29 *Giant* star
30 Weather eye
32 Pen mom
33 Valued violin
34 L.A. campus
35 Sizzling site
36 A few laughs
39 Actress Falana
41 Queen Victoria's granddaughter
42 Mill man
44 ... a *Cheers* star acting like a stud?
47 Plants used in shampoos
48 Smidge
49 Headstone inscription
50 Surfer's pals
51 Trailer puller
53 "Thereby hangs ___"
55 Erechtheum esses
58 Cable car's turnaround
59 Na Na preceder
60 Grimm grotesque
62 Tokyo sport
63 By way of
66 ... actress Jane in a cheesy outfit?
70 Ft. ___, N.J.
71 Staring pair
73 Drug VIP
74 Yug. neighbor
75 Firepower?
77 1940 tune, "___ Cannonball"
79 NL Western Division player
81 Most exalted, in Mexico
84 "Holy moly!"
86 Monterrey uncle
87 French possessive
88 "___ think so"
90 ... the Impaler looking a little battered?
94 Gat
95 Moths with wing eyespots
96 Town near Caen, France
97 Satisfactory
98 Dog or scoundrel
99 Sutter's Mill find, to Luis
100 Bumbling bunch?
102 Claw-foot item
104 Hawn-Gibson film, *Bird on* ___
106 Not to
107 Cal or Texas follower
108 Watergate judge
111 "___ said before ..."
112 High, shallow fly ball
113 Help-offering comment
115 ... an actress saying, "You like me (honk!), you really like me"?
118 *Home Journal* readership
119 ... a baseball star of high caliber?
120 Painter Édouard
121 Secluded corner
122 Lili St. ___
123 Roguish

DOWN

1 Consequently
2 Magnet or pheromone
3 Author Anya
4 Music notes
5 Bullet-train taker, perhaps
6 "I ___ with my own eyes!"
7 Little one
8 Island where Marcos died
9 Very, *non*?
10 Actresses Best and Purviance
11 Teak alternative
12 Goddess of discord
13 Early man?
14 Really cheap, as a stamp
15 ... a Bloom in wet soil?
17 A long way
18 Sidelined
20 Verdi opera
21 She had hissy hair
23 Rescue reward
27 Alchemist's quest
30 Megadeath madness
31 Taken, in a way
33 Name in N.Y.C. restaurant lore
35 Donna of *Saturday Night Fever* and TV's *Angie*
37 ... an ex-candidate being taken for granite?
38 Land east of the Urals
40 Ruins through bungling
43 Duck or color
44 Roof sealant
45 Poise
46 Photo originals
48 Hitchcock film
52 Plaything place
53 "So!"
54 Mind's I
56 Guy de Maupassant rogue, Bel ___
57 Name of two baseball teams
59 Layers
61 Groucho in *Duck Soup*, ___ T. Firefly
63 Take an oath
64 *Mad About You* cousin
65 ... a columnist who wouldn't talk?
67 Listening device
68 Drink with rarebit
69 Stranger
72 Egypt's Port ___
76 Swan lady
78 Charley horse
80 Italian film producer's first name
81 Go out with
82 Vehicle fleet, on the base
83 In a burdensome manner
85 Earthiest, as language
87 Air lanes
89 ___ l'oeil
90 Volunteer org. estab. in '64
91 Poet Amy or Robert
92 Decant
93 Its mbrs. get free maps
94 Shade
98 Like fresh celery
101 Role for Valerie
103 Buffalo
105 Singer of sewing fame
106 Pays
108 Hook's sidekick
109 Roman statesman
110 Member of the chorus
112 Movie ratings
114 Take all the marbles
116 "Mighty ___ a Rose"
117 Invisible cushion?

ACROSS

1 Marks for Marcel
8 Phone trio
11 Surrounded by
15 Fields and Handy
18 *Pinocchio* author
19 Gaucho's water source
20 1960s album, "A Whole ___ Schifrin Goin' On"
21 Loud encouragement
22 Psychoanalyzes press agents?
25 Alice's troubadour
26 The Christian, for one
27 Old Pepsodent rival
28 Rallying cry of the Truck Stop Avengers?
30 Computer-screen symbol
31 *Bin* kin, in Berlin
32 Puccini heroine
34 Types
35 Sometimes twisted anatomy
36 Above, to a bard
37 Florida, to retirees
40 Typical *Death Wish* villains
42 Italian cigarette company?
47 Christening sites
51 Grindable beefs
52 Closing hr., often
54 The Atlas of Afr., e.g.
55 Mars, *e.g.*
56 Name or knife preceder
57 Gas or elec. supplier
59 Wizard's introduction
61 Losing propositions?
62 Certain tackles in the All-Choirboys Football League?
65 TNT start
66 *Peter Pan* girl
67 Writer Henry criticizes a President?
71 Ground
73 Orinoco shocker
74 Typical Moe-Larry-Curly greetings?
78 Michelangelo sculpture
79 Blood brother?
81 Lucy's love
82 Gun site
83 Actor Tamiroff
84 Bold bird
85 Of a leg bone
88 Actress Bethune or tennis star Garrison
89 Landers on lakes
92 Weasellike babes in the woods?
95 Winter Palace residents
96 Shiite's God
98 Cheerleader characteristic
99 Chocolate sub
101 Gam cover
103 Of heartbeats
106 Belief ending
109 Valhalla cheese
110 What Liszt always bragged he could eat, organ-playing-wise?
113 "... who lived in ___"
115 Fabulous bird
116 Kangaroo or Kirk: abbr.
117 Your one-stop friar-costume headquarters?
119 The first life preserver?
120 Bay or gray follower
121 SSTs cross it
122 Some dope
123 *Miz* or *Six* opener
124 John Elroy Sanford, familiarly
125 It's in the bag
126 Saddle-stitching place

DOWN

1 When 32 Across kills Scarpia
2 The K-9 or the Peace
3 Sole extension, sometimes
4 ___ vital
5 Makes marginalia
6 Play climaxes, briefly
7 Goes (through) meticulously
8 Aqueduct feature
9 Tour de France need
10 "Heavy, man"
11 Partner of 29 Down
12 Winner of seven gold medals in 1972
13 Society's woes
14 See 30 Down
15 Why Tarzan never sits on his oboe?
16 Actress Kane
17 Ladd role
23 Address: abbr.
24 Cossack chief
29 Cry of woe
30 With 14 Down, a Jimmy Durante tune
33 Slap-shooting legend
35 A single one
36 Passing marks
38 TNT finish
39 House location?
41 Good times
42 Hemingway sobriquet
43 Skater's feat
44 Buck minus 99
45 Where 33 Down played
46 Extracts venom from
48 Blue Cross, for one: abbr.
49 Responsibility
50 Leaking sound
53 Cleo's guy
57 Marshall Plan's offering
58 Mac toppers
60 *Wayne's World* star Myers
61 City in India
63 1968 Heisman winner
64 With "ball," an arcade game
66 Blows away, figuratively
68 Digs of twigs
69 Camp David pact signer
70 Shampoo brand
71 Finish, as pottery
72 Stunt flying?
75 Leno book, *Leading with My* ___
76 Neck ache
77 Curative cities
78 German article
79 Flabellate
80 Caustic cleaner
84 Plath's *The Bell* ___
86 Indian org.
87 *Cogito*
88 Pizazz
90 Where rats are guinea pigs
91 Obi
93 CFCs watchdog
94 Skin pigment
97 Rice's *The Vampire* ___
99 Reef denizen
100 Love
102 Eightsome
104 Hypo units
105 Pulsate
106 "___ when that happens"
107 Cobbler, at times
108 Like drawn-out divorces
110 Unfurnished
111 Stringed instrument
112 Sch. in the smog
114 Burg, to a Boer
116 Showroom star
118 Pointed-roof covering

ACROSS

1 Given to giving orders
6 War-loving goddess
10 Poet at Bill's inauguration
14 Tear down (its homophone means the opposite)
18 Truly ticked off
19 Tableland
20 Accumulated, as a bill
21 Extra dry
22 "___ ... my least favorite movie"
24 Where to vow to your partner
25 Smaller size
26 Criticize mercilessly
27 ___ huff
28 "___ ... thud!"
31 Directed skyward
34 Baked good
35 Org. for moles?
36 "___ ... and with good reason"
44 Take back (your words)
45 Bauxite, e.g.
46 Stark from Randy Andy's past
47 Big turnoff?
48 Mighty
50 On the subject of
52 According to
53 Tennis star
54 Promotional product
55 "___ ... that's what the studio should order"
60 Minderbinder of *Catch-22*
63 Revival prefix
64 Carriage for Boris
65 Shaggy Tibetan
67 Too
69 "___ ...sure seemed that way, all right"
74 Some dwellers in Wellington
75 And the like: abbr.
76 More muumuulike
77 Invertible palindromic cry
78 Bk. before Job
81 "___ ... my sentiments exactly"
85 Drift, as of events
87 Hillbilly possessive
89 Tiebreaking periods: abbr.
90 Garbage vessel
92 Supercollider tidbit
93 Mountain lake
94 Co-founder of TriStar Pictures
95 Small working part
98 Shearing subject
99 "___ ... but not this one"
104 Respond "like a rug"
105 Hockey legend
106 Parent sub for a night
107 "___ ... on a scale of 1-to-10"
113 It's looking at you, kid
114 The goldfish in *Pinocchio*
118 Broadway beginning
119 Parrying weapons
120 "___ ... my attention"
123 "Get away!"
124 Of ___ (somewhat)
125 Spanish artist Joan
126 Path to "I do"
127 Boys or Boom
128 Addition place
129 Pre-teeners' sch.
130 Strike-zone boundary

DOWN

1 Son of Willy Loman
2 Like slander, as opposed to libel
3 Miss Toga?
4 Delay bedtime
5 Desire
6 Arise (from)
7 Launder again
8 "Love ___ two-way street"
9 Simon follower
10 Seasickness, to Cousteau
11 Starting bet
12 Basic monetary unit of China
13 Fruit with a pit
14 Went on a tear
15 "Eri tu," for one
16 Penultimate element
17 Do a dele?
20 Demi-diameters
23 Kitchen device for a gambler?
29 Working on
30 Russian space station
32 Mideast grp.
33 "Watch yourself now"
36 Small green thing in your soup
37 Whence the Magi came
38 Sgt. Snorkel's dog
39 One-third of a war movie
40 Test
41 Poodle's name
42 First game
43 Torn from today's headlines
49 Agreeable, to teens
51 Frolicking fish-lover
52 Emperor's dog, perh.
53 Type of Bags or rags
56 Tom's role on Roseanne's show
57 Fertile loam
58 Bob Randall play, *6 Rms ___ Vu*
59 *Twin Peaks* creator
61 Dogie catcher
62 It means "bone"
66 Metric weights
68 Factory
69 Gauguin's getaway
70 Jinx
71 Collar-and-tailcoat college
72 Sotheby's signals
73 Sea salt?
74 Manny of baseball
79 "Fancy ___!"
80 "Java" trumpeter
82 Asian desert
83 Bakery topper
84 1963 book by Bob Hope, ___ *Russia $1,200*
86 Photog's soak
88 Nap takers
91 Name that's almost a direction
93 Any and all responsibility
94 Munich mister
95 The world of metropolises
96 Eightsome
97 Phone co.
100 Scram, on the range
101 *Scent of a Woman* director Martin, or a French city
102 Journalist Salinger
103 Waif
107 In the cellar
108 Come again?
109 Stash
110 Church section
111 Illuminating subject?
112 Mild exclamation
115 Escape from, as trackers
116 It vies with *Vogue*
117 Feats of Keats
121 Trouble
122 Table wood

34 Just a Super Guy

...No matter what, it'll end in a tie

ACROSS

1 Bonneville Salt Flats state
5 Burns on *M*A*S*H*, e.g.
8 Lucite layer
12 ___ Raton
16 A handful, maybe
17 Jerk's work
18 A fairy-tale beginning
19 Cow or sow
21 Gift for a dad who's a British sports fan?
24 Peaceful women, perhaps
25 1988 Olympics site
26 Outback critter
27 Containing tin
29 Gift for a firefighting dad?
34 As ___ say (implying)
35 Like many silent comedies
36 Big movie-biz union
37 When Aïda dies
39 Retreat for dad
40 Make ___ (fly over)
43 Actor Howard
45 "Super" film size
48 Gift for a poker-playing dad?
52 Tree-lined st.
53 Pear variety
55 Marina ___, Calif.
56 Warming phenomenon in the Pacific
59 Hubbub
60 "Well, ___ the lucky one!"
62 Actress Valli of *Third Man* fame
63 Case for a lawyer?
65 Mr. Peepers taught it: abbr.
66 Gift for an astronomer dad?
70 These, to Yves
71 Maker of Chatty Cathy
73 Chevalier costar, 1958
74 Becomes weatherworn
76 Cooper's tool
77 At the ___ a hat
79 Sign on a Hertz truck
81 Put through a kitchen device
83 "___ Buttermilk Sky"
84 Gift for a bodybuilding dad?
89 Coal product
90 Last syllable of a word
93 Act introducer
94 Lunch time
95 Tie or track
97 Discotheque description
99 Vacation bookings
101 Money mkt., e.g.
103 Gift for an auto-racing dad?
108 Scrolled Japanese wall hanging
110 Island neckwear
111 Daytime soap
112 O'Neill title word
113 Gift for an actor dad?
119 Went quickly
120 Mr. Rubik
121 Author Kingsley
122 *Music Man* state
123 Goldilocks met *tres* of them
124 Color man?
125 "Prufrock" penner: inits.
126 Acme

DOWN

1 Mark McGwire's alma mater
2 Hard-to-climb hill
3 Cherbourg chum
4 Cartoon magpie
5 The Bates, e.g.
6 Loser to Dwight twice
7 ___ alai
8 Spotlight sharer, in a way
9 With bread as a bed
10 Great one
11 Worded like a telegram
12 Klee Museum city
13 Scary 1978 sequel, *Damien—___*
14 Gift for a mechanic dad?
15 Unalaska denizen
17 A slave, not a wave
19 Megaflop
20 Renamed oil co.
22 Cigarette brand
23 Smear on the Crisco
28 *Treasure of Sierra Madre* author B. ___
29 That bleeping droid
30 Big Stuf cookie
31 Host who's into funny headlines
32 Not quite right
33 Lanai
38 Song syllable
40 Counting everything
41 Jewish festival
42 Enzyme ending
44 Down, a spa; up, artless
46 Peat and Spanish
47 Thinks
49 Rapturous rhyme
50 Perch for the undecided
51 Bear market frenzy
54 Org. that pads its membership?
57 House debt
58 "___ Rainbow"
60 Nova Scotia, once
61 Gift for a hotel clerk dad?
62 Intro to bat or phobia
64 Something to waft over me
65 Agent 86
67 Popular lab bacillus
68 Surveyor's aide
69 Logic
72 Hee or vee preceder
75 "___ Bones"
78 Like Humpty Dumpty's luck
79 Swab anew
80 Not counting: abbr.
82 One of Richelieu's titles, in French
85 Runs
86 Hairy prefix
87 Petropartnership, briefly
88 Russian city
91 Loch of song
92 Wrinkle
96 From ___ stern
98 "___ the money, two ..."
99 "O woe ___!"
100 Coliseums (Latin plural)
101 Feel like ___ again
102 Chocoholic's bean
104 Edged (out)
105 Dutch cheeses
106 Kid on *My Three Sons*
107 Rowan and Marino
109 Fannie and Ginnie, e.g.
114 Ironic
115 Bob or Tom?
116 Bounce
117 Speechlessness
118 See 65 Down

ACROSS

1 "This looks like a ___ for Superman"
4 Andy's young un, casually
7 Floor for axels
10 "Rock-Hard ___ in Just 8 Weeks!"
13 Ex-Clinton Cabinet member
17 Gold in them there *cerros*
18 Pronto
19 Flagstaff AZ campus
20 Jon Lovitz cartoon series
22 Decline
23 What Superman's tailor might spend?
26 Man of Steel ability?
28 Run distance
29 Slangy sailor
30 Put into effect, as a law
31 Fold twice
35 Big leagues
38 Homer's home
40 Sermon coda, "Let ___"
41 Siskel and Ebert sample
42 Largemouth
45 Gem from Australia
47 Rodin's thinker?
48 Florida Stater
50 June 1998 marked Superman's ___ birthday
53 Major port of Mozambique
55 Strand
56 Actress Cates
58 Friend of Fran
61 Show woe
63 Krypton's is 36: abbr.
64 River and WWI battlesite
65 Military region
66 *Hud* director Martin
68 Mainz man
70 Offed, in the Bible
72 Main Mongol
73 "Ain't That" this
75 He had morals
79 Number of *huevos* in an omelet, perhaps
81 U.S. broadcast in Eur.
82 Carnival characters
83 It means "false"
84 Hourly, in Rome
86 Raison ___
88 Superman's 26 Across can't penetrate it
89 Idle, as a machine
92 Halting word
94 *The NeverEnding Story* author
96 Assassin Princip was one
97 Chills
98 A Yale song contains a lot of them
100 Harbor scooper
104 Waif
106 No. 1
108 Old Chinese weight
110 Mauna ___
111 Tense
112 Going by Lois at the *Daily Planet*?
115 Peek, Superman-style?
119 Cat's dog
122 Matchbox toys
123 Broadcast
124 Giant standout
125 Nev. neighbor
126 Vostok launcher
127 Vacation time, in Paris
128 Inalienable items: abbr.
129 Leak sound
130 Superman is lifting one on the cover of *Action Comics* No. 1 (1938)

DOWN

1 Superman co-creator Shuster (with Jerry Siegel)
2 Royal symbol
3 Hope and Hoskins
4 Roughly even
5 Actor who seems perfect to play Superman?
6 Pitcher
7 Illustrator's renderings
8 Rich salad
9 Sister of Teddy
10 Philip who played Master Kan on *Kung Fu*
11 Barbara's *Beaches* costar
12 List of events
13 With 130 Across in mind, what Superman might do as an encore?
14 Hellenic H
15 Small drink
16 Snoopy's WWI persona
20 907.18 kilograms
21 Janet, Jean, and Kelly
24 Role(s) for Joanne
25 Lavish affection (on)
27 More land
31 House mbr.
32 Superman's first urge every time he comes to a door?
33 Opposite of long.
34 Pinkerton symbol
35 Escher and Hammer
36 Mugful for Muggeridge
37 Impatient words from Lois to a colleague?
39 Leonard, Myron, and William
43 Sans date
44 Mantilla wearers
46 Nancy Hanks's kid
49 Arms assn.
50 Two hours before prime time
51 "___ wise guy!"
52 Chamois's perch
54 U2 Incident figure
57 Hearing aid company
59 Do nothing
60 British composer Thomas
61 Rocky eminence
62 Hilltop
65 Something Superman doesn't do, since they just bounce off?
67 How to make the star of TV's *Superman* into the star of filmdom's *Superman*?
69 Fisherman, at times
71 Something wrong
74 Arizona's zone: abbr.
76 Take to court
77 Room guarded by eunuchs
78 Group of whales
80 ___ Lanka
83 Pocket protector item
85 "Do you have Prince Albert ___?" (old phone gag)
87 Oil or coal, e.g.
90 ___ generis (unique)
91 Poetic time of day
92 Pugilistic org.
93 Half of a chocolate drink
95 Carson's carcinogen
96 Some promgoers
99 Beggar boy in a TV opera
101 Where David met Goliath
102 Bust, as an attorney
103 Like pre-electricity lamps
105 Formal insult fests
107 Summer ermine
109 Wildebeest
112 Movie ratings
113 All-purpose army folks: abbr.
114 Big picture?
115 Mustangs' campus
116 Canon camera type
117 Wynn et al.
118 Text ending?
120 Nabokov work
121 It kicks the L out of "glory"

ACROSS

1 Out of alignment
5 Bryn ___
9 Hand holders?
13 Koi or gripe
17 Sung soliloquy
18 Competition foil
19 Console features
21 Original *Videos* host Bob
22 Help you can drop
23 Speaker of baseball
24 Near, as beer
25 Sadistic
26 You've seen it on *America's Funniest Home Videos*
30 Scoreless football game, perhaps
31 "___ little rusty ..."
32 Orgy regular
33 See 26 Across
43 That boat
44 Presuming that
45 "I can ___ all now ..."
46 Boys Town st.
47 Make into a statute
49 On strike
52 Twenty-cup server
53 Schmoozefest
56 See 26 Across
61 Slipknotted apparel
62 Philippine shoe queen
63 Western Arizonan
64 Mun. Code item
65 Very soft, to a virtuoso
66 Actors Dick and Susannah
69 Brunch time
70 Opposite of rej.
73 Former U.S. $10 gold coin
75 Tijuana time-out
77 Cold, in Cuernavaca
78 See 26 Across
83 Korea's former name
84 Lady of Sp.
85 ___-wop music
86 Sour in taste
87 Mineral ___
88 Surface holes
90 *The Day of the Locust* author
93 Alfonso's aunt
94 See 26 Across
101 Ethiopian of puzzledom
102 Time enough to evolve a little
103 Crooner Redbone
104 See 26 Across
112 *Beau* ___
113 Ooze
114 Hardly any effort at all
115 Site of *mon oncle*'s monocle
117 Las Vegas and Palm Springs
118 Occupied
119 Maple genus (or one who cruises through a test?)
120 Zip, to Zapata
121 Dump emanation
122 The ___ room
123 Sanguine
124 Prepare prunes

DOWN

1 Dickensian exclamation
2 Olympian Heiden
3 Name that Hirschfeld hides in his caricatures
4 Arm art
5 Ways
6 Based on logic
7 Gewürztraminer, to a German
8 Pass over again
9 Shelley's elegy to Keats
10 Engagement clincher
11 *Gunsmoke* guy
12 Serb, for one
13 Part of a woman's juggling act
14 Water, to Juanita
15 There's film all over it
16 Disgraced TV club
20 Apathy opposite
21 Cancel a mission
27 Burger option
28 Little dickens
29 Crisis call
33 Elvis hit, "In the ___"
34 Painter Auguste or director Jean
35 Opined sonorously
36 ___ mind (in agreement)
37 Nine, in Nice
38 Former Spice Girl Halliwell
39 Donkey and stallion's offspring
40 Almanac guts
41 Lacking a charge
42 Low level
48 Tape alternatives: abbr.
50 Clock-stopping
51 Agenda infinitive
53 "___-you-are"
54 The face ___ angel
55 Com or fat preceder
57 Crude street weapon
58 Insinuate
59 Language of Iran
60 ___-frutti
65 Lobby announcement
67 Variety
68 Utah lily
70 Gulf War reporter Peter
71 Orange acid
72 Old quarter of Algiers
73 Harris and Sullivan
74 Shiner over Mexico
76 Demonstrated
77 Simile start?
78 Plain Dealer's state
79 Lounge (about)
80 Major players who know the score: abbr.
81 Munro's *nom*
82 ___ of the arts
83 Wheel tooth
88 Lois Lane's paper
89 Supreme Court justice appointed by Ford
91 French churches
92 Tourist's eyeful
95 "C'mon! Giddyap!"
96 Flea attacks
97 Bother
98 Body extreme
99 "Parking ___"
100 Burger option
104 Sweat unit
105 Ex-name of Exxon
106 Test
107 (To) microwave: slang
108 First murder scene
109 Steve Martin's Texas birthplace
110 Nifty
111 Nobel-winning author of *The Counterfeiters*
112 Petroleum, e.g.
116 Murphy has one

ACROSS

1 Fermat's forte, briefly
5 Ground gripper for the Gipper
10 Fiver face
13 Diving bird
18 Return one's call?
19 Marilyn of the Met
20 Bathtub booze
21 Violin precursors
23 Bad-marriage movie of 1991?
26 Nutrition pioneer Davis
27 Departure party
28 Your favorite piece of geometric art?
30 Cartoon-page exclamation
31 Broad cast?
34 Free
35 Frozen *wasser*
36 Yesterday's
38 Actor from Mysore, India
39 Guy who's the life of the party?
43 Easter, for one: abbr.
44 Sites for shackles
46 Letters before *Arizona* or *Pueblo*
47 Charlie and Pete
48 "Ah so," for example?
51 Sleight maneuver
52 Missile crisis "blinker"
53 Orléans outburst
54 Simpson on sax
55 Org. that grabbed Patty
58 Central Poland city
60 Marlon fights him in *On the Waterfront*
62 Like numbers rackets?
65 They're conceivable
67 Coping device
69 Spooner was one: abbr.
70 Get around
71 More macho writer?
75 Smile with pride
78 ___ instant
79 Pompeii portraits
80 Cordelia's dad
81 ___ for effort
83 Line for Willard Scott
85 Panama palindrome, partly
86 Chef's overreaction to a little criticism?
90 On ___ (carousing)
92 Garlic, to García
94 Get bullish
95 Mystery-craftin' Grafton
96 Chinese restaurant owner?
98 See 9 Down
99 *Town Without ___*
100 Author Levin
101 ___ gallop
102 Clinton pal Panetta
103 Oft-numbered work
105 Tom Thumb attire?
110 Couch potato's problem
113 Very, to Brits
114 Savings?
118 Cosine reciprocal
119 Arts-funding org.
120 Composer Berg
121 "What's ___ for me?"
122 Some terriers
123 Soviet place name abbr.
124 Sweetbread
125 Singer James

DOWN

1 World Series winners in 1969 and 1986
2 Tylenol target
3 Foul-mouthed hockey team?
4 "Stop!"
5 Rub the wrong way
6 Goldbrick
7 West addition?
8 *Et*
9 With 98 Across, an early orbiter
10 Malaria symptom
11 European-style cafes
12 The major feud groups?
13 Mom's mom, affectionately
14 Funny Foxx
15 Salon celeb José
16 "We're ready to ___ you" (the Ghostbusters' motto)
17 Filled pastries
22 Rhyme or reason
24 ___ the floor with
25 Photo ___ (press events)
29 Like Oscar and Felix
31 Sid's brother?
32 Contribute to crime
33 Savage breast soother
36 Film, in *Variety*
37 It's from the bottom of my hearth
38 Ray, the swimmer
39 Third-year student
40 Get the lead out
41 To fly, in Florence
42 Discrimination ending
44 Ham container?
45 Doogie portrayer ___ Patrick Harris
49 Native ruler of Hyderabad (anagram of MAINZ)
50 A, B, ___ (multiple choice)
51 Dickens orphan
54 Occurrence at Make-Out Point?
55 Able to keep a straight face around Freberg?
56 Swan lady
57 Mideast gulf
58 Ms. Wertmuller
59 Evidence of decay
61 Airline to the Orient
63 Bird's beak
64 Of birds
66 Pale yellow, as a complexion
68 Rope, revolver, or candlestick
72 "Peachy keen"
73 Exclamation of frustration
74 Microscopic "messenger"
76 Michaelmas daisy, e.g.
77 Mineral hardness scale
82 Ouzo flavoring
84 Wager
85 *Invasion of the Body Snatchers* prop
87 Fascinated by
88 Snip
89 Crucial
90 Gets in
91 Township near Hackensack
92 Reaches
93 Worley et al.
96 High-pitched instruments
97 Day break
99 Cleavon Little's 1970 Tony role
102 Baton Rouge sch.
103 Upright
104 Chest muscle, at the gym
106 Battleship color
107 Old slave
108 Decomposes
109 Pre-1917 power broker
110 Section of Sammy's autobio
111 Onomatopoetic: abbr.
112 Mystery dog
115 Newspaper
116 ___ along (the whole time)
117 Hoop grp.

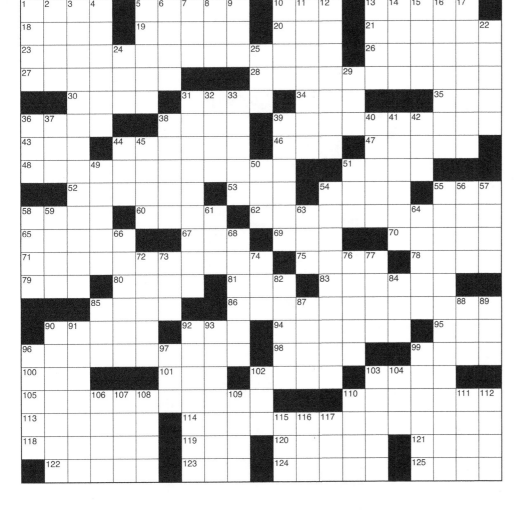

ACROSS

1 Top-of-the-line
7 Redness exemplar
11 Tranquillity Base transit
15 Word on a bulb
19 Plagiarized
20 Carbon and Iron are two of its counties
21 Song for Don José
22 Zeno's place
23 Eastwood discussing his bloodier movies?
25 Zsa Zsa on darning socks?
27 Eating reminder
28 Stubby end
29 Reason for Madonna's bathroom clog?
31 Killy event
34 Come-ons, of a sort
35 Dash
36 Flu, mono, etc.?
40 Contact cleaner suffix
41 Speed instrument, briefly
45 The dog's problem in *Turner and Hooch*
46 "Camptown Races" horse
47 Italian possessive
48 Home near Nome
49 "___ to Pieces"
50 Melmac wiseguy
53 Reason the Parks Service outlawed Pictionary picnics?
57 Main thing that happens in David Mamet movies?
60 Seuss character, Sam-___
61 Back on a bark
62 Puck stopper
63 N.J. neighbor
64 Period for Pedro
65 Fritters (away)
67 Number of coins in *la fontana*
69 Story of a comedian before he switched instruments?
74 Call off
75 The ___ Marbles
76 Improve, perhaps
77 One antacid
79 "The" end
82 Actress Ruby
84 Slangy money
85 "You mean," ___, "I'm gonna be in *The Godfather*?!"
88 Famous scene in *Fiddler Crab on the Roof*?
93 Ransom's baby
94 Serengeti beast
95 The British Isles, for one
96 "___ reconsidered"
97 Label
99 Paintings by Paul
101 China-Korea border river
102 Leader of the pack, perhaps
103 Oil shortage?
107 Gilda's Wawa
109 Chinese Casanova, maybe
110 George Washington portraitist
111 First thing you learn in vase class?
114 Ugh relative
115 "Test's over!"
119 Spend time with *The Quayle Crayon Book*?
120 Sequel to the film *Thug Takes a Vacation*?
124 Wait on the line
125 Fight night site
126 Word over a door
127 Puget Sound port
128 She, in Florence
129 When most people work
130 Mauritius sight, once
131 Astaire and Hugo

DOWN

1 Letters on Sputnik
2 Showgirl in Manilow's "Copacabana"
3 Hear ___ drop
4 Serenades
5 Unshakable
6 A word for God
7 Insecticide
8 WWII theater
9 Turned on one's ___
10 Casey was at it
11 He looked mahvelous
12 "Able was I ___ ..." (palindrome start)
13 Home of Lake Wobegon
14 Hopalong's sit-upon
15 "___ on together ..." (line from "Suspicious Minds")
16 Jai ___
17 Crockett's birthpl.
18 Make, as doilies
24 Amounting to zip
26 Rainy-day acct.
30 They're on the infrastructure repair list: abbr.
32 Dey job, once
33 Samoa studier Margaret
36 Mus. chord
37 Exhorted
38 *60 Minutes* curmudgeon
39 Scorsese's alma mater, briefly
40 Combustion need
42 He's Thicke
43 Fuel or drink
44 Oprah or Rosie
47 Playwright-director David
48 Words said over a drumroll
51 Hero's girl
52 Dracula's pain in your neck
54 Home delivery person?
55 Late actress Ina
56 "One ___ days, Alice ..."
58 Gin fruit
59 Apple or capital
65 Ft. Knox bar
66 Carpet style
68 Folies Bergère designer, once
70 Remove a beaver's work
71 How Lindy did it
72 Floor for a spore?
73 Elbower
78 Painter Édouard
79 "No matter how hard ___ ..."
80 Strawberry's field, once
81 One of three squares?
83 Parts of sacs around hearts
86 Fireplace prop
87 Luxuriant
89 Tom Collins ingredient
90 Memorable role for Anne Baxter
91 Wd. after bike or business
92 Reacts to a long, hard day
98 Argued heatedly about
100 Trellis, often
102 On
103 Coal measure
104 Monopolized, in a way
105 Pinch from a chain reaction
106 North or South place
108 Great Rift Valley's loc.
109 First Oscar film
111 Contented comments
112 Social woes
113 Lots
116 Valentino, once
117 Roz Russell role
118 Young hawk, in falconry
119 Ernesto Guevara
121 Tic-tac-toe line
122 Planet's end
123 Penrod, for one

ACROSS

1 "Oh no," to Ohm
4 Darjeeling break
11 Arena feature, often
15 "Alas!"
19 Refuges from sun or rain (4)
21 Birth of a notion
22 Gusto
23 It's up in lights (5)
24 Ishtar tried to seduce him (4)
26 They have bad habits
27 A new homophone?
28 Timing abbr.
29 ___ Lena (affectionate term for an old boat)
30 Labor leader Eugene
31 Every last bit
33 Go ___ (fight)
35 German article
36 A revived version of
37 Drove slowly
40 Test of a sort
42 Sashimi lover's sash
44 What *-ation* means
47 CSA defender
48 Aleutian island
50 Pot pie morsel
52 Waffle brand
55 Roebling feat, 1869-83 (4)
59 Lamaze has one
61 Workers' ___ (type of insurance)
62 Saint, in Rio
63 "... ___ happy new year"
64 Artist's colors
65 Typist's asset
67 At General Mills, it "stands for goodness"
69 Role for Clark
71 Emerg. call
72 Near-obsession (6)
77 Cent preceder
80 Cease, at sea
81 Acceptable: slang
82 Prize founder
86 Stuck
88 Chamber effect
90 Afros and beehives
93 Agenda heading
94 "Whether 'tis ___ ..."
95 Radio-TV jargon (8)
98 Exile isle
99 Proposition vote
101 Cameo style
102 Chinese concept
103 Japanese lettuce, perhaps
104 Problem child?
106 Earvin's nickname
108 Champagne cooler (or a fat rap star?)
111 Country pops
113 Burma's first P.M.
115 Perform without ___
117 Operator info: abbr.
118 Kirlian phenomenon
122 Off the boat
124 Soc. or league
125 Collegian Bush, e.g.
127 Main monk
128 Open, Closed, or Bus. Hours (6)
130 With 135 Across, a British pub request (9)
133 Drink to excess, old-style
134 Rent
135 See 130 Across
136 War god
137 The fat of the lamb
138 Hurled anew
139 1992 Kentucky Derby winner Lil E. ___

DOWN

1 Clear ___ (not clear)
2 Jurist Salmon or Samuel
3 Mt. Sinai, in the Bible
4 Greek crosses
5 Shearing candidate
6 Fuel finale
7 Pins-and-needles feeling
8 ___ instant (pronto)
9 Merged film co.
10 Language ending
11 Individual numbers
12 Head Norse?
13 Velvet Fog's first name
14 1969 moon lander
15 Emerald City princess
16 Letterman's times (6)
17 Actor Davis
18 Cultural prefix
20 Followers of "N-O"?
25 Plane prefix, formerly
28 Sum things wrong
31 Feats on ice
32 OPEC member
34 Gambling (4)
35 Salon buy
38 It had Ham in it
39 Bit of goo
41 Crazy, in a phrase
43 Brest beast
44 Early recitation
45 Rider's prop
46 Thousand-pager, usually
49 Lieutenant on *Perry Mason*
51 Nicola of Cremona
53 ___ the dogs
54 Laudatory lit
56 Page for polit. cartoons
57 *Ora pro* ___ (pray for us)
58 *Anna Christie* star, 1930
60 Singer John
64 Rub the right way
66 Hang loosely
68 Bury
70 Poet Doolittle
73 Africa's ___ Coast
74 Brewery vessel
75 Capricious
76 Answer to the Little Red Hen's plea
77 Maine, the ___ Tree State
78 Organic compound (or "unaccompanied" backwards)
79 Popular Jewish soap opera? (6)
83 Too thin
84 Competitive zeal
85 Bird or birdbrain
87 Bridge coup
89 Bird's or baby's sound
91 Porosis preceder
92 Palindromic records
95 Brave, clean, and reverent grp.
96 Roman 111
97 Mary and Murray's boss
100 Winged giant
105 Uncut, in a way
107 January birthstone
109 Certain musical chord
110 Infant in a celebrated surrogate-mother case
111 Rotelle, e.g.
112 Fur company founder
114 Aeries
116 Plains abode
119 *Lusitania* sinker
120 Way to go
121 "... a poem lovely as ___"
123 40 Across specimens
124 Grimm heavy
126 Santa makes one
127 ___ *Good Men*
129 Debtor's letters
130 Smaller, as some dicts.
131 Slangy seagoer
132 Song-ending shout, in Sonora

ACROSS

1 *Beauty and the Beast*'s beauty (1991)
6 Paris suburb
10 Afterthought No. 2
13 "Buy Me Love" beginner
17 A Begley or a Chaney
18 Clinic or spread
19 Tiny tax shelter
20 Wahine's ta-ta
22 Apple-pie order?
25 Sir, if you're under a punkah
26 Bach's "Little Fugue ___ Minor"
27 Stack film
28 Numerical order?
30 Peking addition
31 Bean town?
33 Free-form concert
35 Q-U filling
36 Light into
38 Pecking order?
42 Hambletonian pace
45 Retireemobiles
46 Conformist's adverb
47 Long fellow of the sea
48 Euclid's love: abbr.
49 True-blue
51 FFA interest
54 Stash of cash
56 Littler guy with the Force
58 Starting stake
60 Dr. Leary's prescription
61 Witness-stand no-no
62 Suborder?
65 "Tipperary" tune start
66 Beetle and Zero: abbr.
68 Teeter-totter half
69 Something to pick
70 *Alien, Aliens,* etc.
72 *Hop on Pop* penner
74 Side order?
79 Anita Hill inquisitor
81 Garr-Keaton comedy
83 NYSE listings
84 American *mer*
86 Victory goddess
87 Confident solver's tool
88 Social order?
93 Order member
94 Noodle warmer
95 Oat or piece follower
96 Spanking support
97 Cleaning cloth
99 Country drs., often
100 "Can ___? Can I? Huh? Please?"
102 Bout endings, briefly
104 Brit. flyers
106 Jolt with juice
108 Pretoria's land: abbr.
109 Let the emotions flow
110 New World Order?
115 Pine spine
117 Type of boss or bull
119 Uncensored
120 Touchstone's play: abbr.
121 "Free will" preceder
122 Alphabetical order?
126 Spear kin
129 Ending for Car, Tom, or Ober
130 15th century date
132 Restraining order?
135 Shoe leather
136 Spoiled one's dinner
137 Charlie Brown's "kite eater"
138 Typo list
139 Stepped
140 The prince or the pauper
141 Egg-shaped
142 Dandelion and darnel

DOWN

1 Spinning top?
2 Elgar's ___ *Variations*
3 Used a fuse
4 Rawls and Reed
5 Mr. Rubik
6 Do Little work
7 Man or woman's nickname
8 Part of CBS: abbr.
9 "___ my special angel ..."
10 Glass lab-tube
11 Sub- or super-, e.g.
12 Rani wrap
13 Docket load
14 In the style of
15 Back order?
16 Money order?
17 Slop
21 First fatality
23 Pearl Harbor attack authorizer
24 Yellowstone and Yosemite: abbr.
29 Large container
32 Colorful hangings
34 Skeptic's outburst
37 Sellout sign
39 Org. or cigarette brand
40 Loathsome ones
41 Trudge
43 It's long and lonesome
44 *Discover*'s pop cousin
48 Actor-turned-envoy John
49 Parasite
50 Mormon letters
51 Edelweiss environs
52 Short order?
53 Mail order?
55 Japan's legislature
57 *Out of Africa* author
59 Sony prods.
63 Car or truck: abbr.
64 Airport abbr.
67 Missile type: abbr.
71 Actor Holm
73 Embattled French river of WWI
75 Henri's here
76 Wallops
77 Wear and tear
78 Bartlett, for one
80 Farm femmes
82 A Pep Boy
85 Astound
87 Greek letter
89 Taxi meter info
90 Peter's *A Shot in the Dark* costar
91 Wax, in Oaxaca
92 Broadcast again
98 Fiero or Fiesta filler
101 Honked off
103 Against
105 Made like a bird
107 Educ. confab
109 Deceit metaphor
110 "___ the rear"
111 Olympics preemptor of the 1940s
112 "Just follow ___"
113 George and T.S.
114 Black-clad martial artist
115 Pseudonyms, briefly
116 Resided
118 Wage-watching agcy.
123 Airline to Israel
124 Big cheese in Athens
125 Continental combiner
127 Had the answer to
128 To be on the Riviera?
131 Short sentence
133 Hawaiian shirt accessory
134 One of the empires: abbr.

ACROSS

1 "What ___ thinking?"
5 Registered symbols: abbr.
8 Crony's conclusion
11 Derive by reasoning
16 The ___ Heights
17 Zip, to Zola
19 Alcohol arrest, briefly
20 Culture that gave us the word "berserk"
21 Washday folks who didn't check their pockets?
24 Oreo filling
25 Makes sure no one steals any Fab or Tide?
26 Was an accessory to
27 Alert from the P.D.
28 Bite aftermath, perhaps
29 Map abbr.
30 Filmed, in *Variety*
32 *David Copperfield* embezzler
34 Class for new Americans: abbr.
36 Sport with belts
37 Water-diluted rum
40 Drops on your head?
43 Four-legged body-surfers
47 Stick around
49 Folks who are serious about cleaning?
52 Bordeaux buddy

53 Lead paint monitor: abbr.
54 Sticker numbers
55 Rotates
56 Composer Khachaturian
57 They're right in front of U
58 Less risky
59 Heavy, as dump trucks
60 She put on a happy face
62 Eastwood apology after opening a running machine?
68 Money maker
69 Take by force
70 20 Across goddess of love and beauty
71 Bird's cry
74 Letters in letters?
75 Ointment
76 Truffaut's *The Story of ___*
77 LBJ VP
78 *Magnum, P.I.*'s setting: abbr.
79 1969 film about people who ruthlessly yank your wash out before it's done?
81 Brontë and Post
83 Of the north wind
84 Singer Marvin
85 Epsilon follower
86 Major work
88 A movie channel, in TV-listing shorthand
90 Wilbur's pet
94 "___ we speak"

96 Harmonizing music, ___-wop
99 Smack or switch add-on
102 Feathered giant
103 Cut in a certain way
105 With 110 Across, what laundromats affect?
109 Maker of the arcade game Missile Command
110 See 105 Across
111 Lacks
112 With Kan, a dog food
113 Like Amahl
114 Actress Rainer
115 McCourt bestseller, *Angela's ___*
116 Company connections
117 Letters after Latvian, once
118 Ailment ending

DOWN

1 "It ___ the first time"
2 *Star Wars* actor's first name
3 Greet, in a way
4 Small bay
5 Axioms
6 Ho Chi follower
7 Passover-eve event
8 The germ of an ___
9 Excess

10 Went wide
11 Cuzco dwellers
12 Ex-strongman of Panama
13 Favorite actor of laundromat owners?
14 Mrs. Hoggett in *Babe*
15 Oboist's need
16 Freak out
18 Orioles' home
21 Exaggerated kiss sound
22 Make ___ (display one's anger loudly)
23 Norma McCorvey, in a famous court case
31 ___ feat (quite an accomplishment)
33 Come before
35 Speaker, in Latin
36 Sammy Davis and Lon Chaney
38 Word of apology
39 Tiny insect
41 "Poor People's March" leader of 1968
42 They, in Nantes
44 Lose on purpose
45 Sampras, for one
46 Hosp. areas
48 Clock info
49 Historically correct, as a jazz arrangement: abbr.
50 Musical cabinet
51 Makes up (for)
52 Come up
54 Greek letter
56 Bowls over
59 "___ you could do it!"
60 Moves like Elvis's hips
61 Blue diamond, for one
63 Quisling's crime
64 "Don't ___ soul"
65 Copyreading instruction
66 They're looking at you, kid
67 Morse bit
71 At the home of
72 Sighing words
73 Result of using too much Clorox?
75 Leb. neighbor
76 *Seven Days in May* actress
79 Trig func.
80 Marketplaces
82 Penny on TV
83 Francis X. of the silents
87 Cuomo's successor
89 Bunnies' boss
91 School break
92 Overact
93 French painter Raoul
95 Checks out books?
96 One behind the wheel: abbr.
97 Trompe l'___
98 Alaskan cruise sights
100 Greek weights
101 "Fish ___ bait"
103 "So funny I forgot to laugh"
104 Landing guesses, briefly
106 Wet wigglers
107 Thanksgiving fare
108 Four, on some old clocks

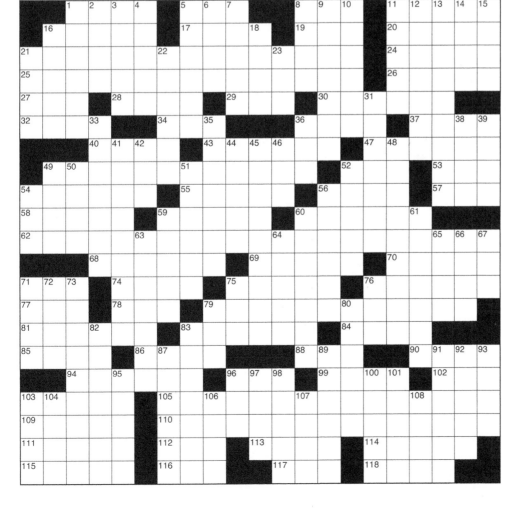

ACROSS

1 Sophocles opus
11 Of bees
16 Ostentatious display
20 Dental floss, for one
21 1961 monster movie
22 Russian city
23 Dangling carrots, perhaps
24 Word in a Fugard title
25 Russian river
26 Comic strip exclamation
27 City on the Rhone
28 Bemused looks
29 San Antonio Peak, formerly
30 Used a prie-dieu
31 Down-home side dish
32 Becomes aware of
33 West African river
36 Dave Garroway's *Today* show signoff
37 Ran after
38 Sartre play, *No ___*
39 Ty Cobb and Al Kaline
41 His day is April 25
43 Home away from home, at times
44 Certain notes
45 Travel like Magellan
46 Adherent's suffix
49 Rachmaninoff work
51 Moonwalker Eugene
53 More, to Moreno
55 Playful fish-eater
56 Scottish town
58 Hungarian dog
59 Phonograph part
60 A *Rocky* or a *Star Trek*
61 Tar
64 Up ___ (100 per cent)
66 Junior Walker's instrument
67 Go downhill
68 Area of San Francisco, ___ Valley
69 Semester tester
71 Tunnels
73 Anesthetic
75 It "blows up real good"
76 Predicament
78 Sipped
81 English *elle*
83 *Fuente* output
84 Dire situation
85 Card table stake
86 Disposes of evidence, perhaps
88 McCartney's *McCartney* album, e.g.
89 Like ___ not
90 Landlord's dictum
92 Errata
94 Namesakes of Alphonse's friend
96 Laments
97 Pulverize
98 Post-jogging sounds
99 Senator Kefauver
100 Israel's foreign minister, 1977-79
101 Connie in *The Godfather*
102 Place for an ace
105 Snobs put them on
106 Embattled Balkans
107 Clavicle
109 God, to Gaius
110 Restaurant sign, "___ Joe's"
111 Burkina Faso, before
112 Puzzle man Rubik
113 *Lycidas*, for one
114 Oliver North's superior, once

DOWN

1 Bee's concern
2 River into Donegal Bay
3 First word in a carol
4 Common contraction
5 Island off the Malay Peninsula
6 Without medical care
7 Type of painting
8 Hold firmly
9 Night times, in ads
10 Poison indicators
11 Mushroom variety
12 Courtesy
13 He played the villain in *Die Hard With a Vengeance*
14 Who-knows-how-long
15 Stats, often: abbr.
16 *The Tenant* director
17 Two-word threat
18 Darned
19 *Luther* and *Sleuth*, e.g.
28 *The Tin Drum* author
29 Campsite invader
30 Kitchen whistler
31 Goldfinger portrayer
32 Clinton Cabinet member
33 Crucial situation, in tennis
34 Huffings and puffings
35 Birthday that's still ten years too early for Willard Scott to notice you
36 Butter ingredient
37 Less-than-sterling grade
40 Smooth-talking
42 Waterproof cover
47 Collide with
48 Passer-turned-pitchman
50 Drives
51 Navigator's place
52 Put the kibosh on
54 Smug ones
57 Brit. letter carrier's stop
62 Crude vehicles
63 "Aromatic" boats
65 Anoints anew
70 Tennyson poem
72 C-rated
74 Black hair, brown eyes, etc.
77 Icer's need
79 *What's My Line?* regular
80 John Lennon book, ___ *in the Works*
82 The quicker waker-upper
84 The Newt Network?
87 Coop group
90 More inclined to listen at doors
91 Beat at a meet
93 Like fresh bread, perhaps
95 "We'll see 'em ___ first" (*King Lear*)
96 Civil War general
97 Follower of "a la"
98 Insect appendages
100 Agreement
101 Ed's mouse
102 Surprise of a sort
103 Grafted, in heraldry
104 Raze, with "down"
106 "Did I tell you?"
107 Thermos top, often
108 Jack's home

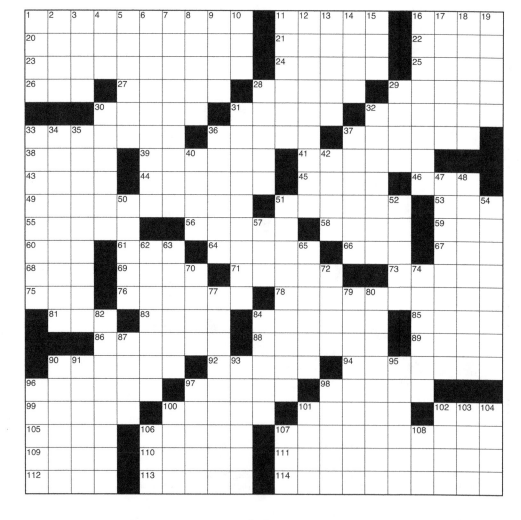

43 The Lost Films of Jerry Lewis*

...Cracking wise

ACROSS

1 He gave the English a lift
5 Members of *Troglodytes troglodytes*
10 Like Godiva
14 Like Godiva?
18 23rd Psalm verb
19 Diplomat, to Dirac
20 Yemen's capital
21 Prizms and Storms
22 Jerry's tall-guy, short-guy comedy?
24 Quotable-notable volume
26 Anagram of 21 Across
27 Jerry's remake of a Victor Herbert work?
29 Tin man?
32 One noted for cutting remarks
33 '60s battle zone
34 Team scream
35 "How can ___ this ..."
36 Poker promises
38 Rap, reggae, or rock: abbr.
40 Compatible mach.
42 Grouper gatherer
43 Jerry's comedy about a hobo who feeds squirrels?
47 Tiny tunnelers
51 Teddy's inits.
52 *The Night of the Hunter* scripter James
53 Encouraged and then some
54 Grape or passion follower
55 Cliff is one, on *Cheers*
57 " ... days ___ September ..."
58 U.S. law (enacted in 1970) aimed at organized crime
60 Go for
61 Hall or Potts
62 He had a hand in Kukla
63 FDR book, with 1 Down
64 It's next to N. Mex.
65 Jerry's *Hamlet*?
70 Shot clock abbr.
72 Rest and restricted, e.g.
73 Legendary potato chip inventor George
74 Jack and Jimmy
77 Tic-tac-toe loser
78 *Mr. Mom* tootsie
79 Ring finales
80 Get
82 Feels the heat
84 Michigan county on Lake Michigan
86 Open, peaty wasteland
87 TV's The ___ Squad
88 Ort entree
89 Jerry's visit-to-a-crazy-planet comedy?
91 A real swingin' grp.
92 Given the nod, in headlines
94 Lay odds
95 Like the biggest airports, briefly
96 Cover
97 *Equus* member
100 Milk-biz org.
102 Say uncle
105 Twirled items
107 With 112 Across, Jerry's comedy about abstract art?
110 Cuttings container
111 Ludlum's *The ___ Inheritance*
112 See 107 Across
116 Land of blarney
117 Football great Ronnie
118 The Colosseum, today
119 Leave out
120 Nighttime host
121 Cafeteria slide-along
122 Matthew Brady shade
123 A, O, or AB

DOWN

1 See 63 Across
2 Greek letter
3 Malice aforethought, e.g.
4 Actor's walk-on?
5 Unites
6 Trenton legislator's I.D.
7 Least crooked
8 A party-pooper
9 Searches meticulously
10 Popular chocolate bar
11 Cartwright in black
12 Showed again
13 Get on board
14 Curved construction
15 Oil giant
16 "Aw, that's a ___ hooey!"
17 Writing competition
23 Notorious Manuel
25 Squirrel perch
28 Turn ___ (lose crunch)
29 Room with a viewing
30 Tarzan's one
31 Jerry's film bio about a singer?
32 Like Lamb Chop
37 The yoke's on them
39 Breastbone
41 Make imperfect
43 Personalized pin-ons
44 Hangings that are hard to watch
45 Jerry's film bio about a sports legend?
46 Typical Lewis character
48 Jerry's comical Indian saga?
49 Torus on a Taurus
50 Hellish river
54 Author's note
56 Repose
57 Crayon choices
59 Team-reduction process
62 Lovable camp invader
63 Burden
66 Chorus syllable
67 Florida bird
68 Loud as lions
69 VCR button
70 Begins the process of
71 Leave the scene
75 Ankle-high work shoe
76 Car styles
79 Made lace
80 Left at sea?
81 Indy safety feature
83 Take ___
85 Eon
86 Blanc, for one
89 Recipe instruction
90 Pilot's shoe?
93 Ex-*New Yorker* critic Pauline
96 Like some movie love scenes
97 Photog Adams
98 Liberator of Venezuela
99 Blotch
101 Rex or Harrison
103 Whopper tellers
104 Result
106 Neckwear or racetrack
108 Bond novel
109 Girl's name ending
110 American Express rival
113 Cuckoo bird (or *Wheel of Fortune* buy)
114 Enjoy liqueur
115 *Printemps* follower

* We hope

ACROSS

1 Type of wolf, not shark
5 Casino equipment
9 Tropical fruits
15 Like a giant squid?
21 First law of astrodynamics, made simple?
23 Make a minister
24 Sends out
25 ___ nutshell
26 One for their side
27 Ansel's orig.
28 Rejections
30 Devil's tail?
31 Canned soup ingredient
32 African antelope
34 Mine matter
36 Gambler's last resort
38 Cheer, or type of beer
40 Greek's H
41 Those !@#$%*! people next door?
49 Slaves
51 Ref. tome
52 Wagon
53 Member of the pod squad
54 Wrath
55 Neckline shape
56 Intro to *Nova*?
58 Woozy
59 Mind game
60 Nixon's Chuck
62 Jabbering jabber, once
63 Spike Lee's *Get on the* ___
65 Serengeti stampeder
66 Real-life reason for some high-level indictments in the late 1980s?
68 Swatter's goal?
72 S.F. time
73 Spectacular span
74 Wartime prez
75 Descendant of an ark passenger
76 Kareem, before
77 Toward the front
79 Hesitation indication
82 Hard drive measure
83 House mbr.
84 Author Levin
85 Independent group
87 John Cusack, to Joan
88 Sweetened
90 The Idi Amin Hall of Fame?
94 Bounce
95 Teen's adjective
96 Salt Lake player
97 Western star Jack
101 40, as opposed to 39
104 Explosive
105 Took off
107 Hardly any taste at all?
110 Lilly of drug fame
111 Future perch
112 A personal question
113 Oscar de la ___
115 Monroe's *Niagara* co-star
117 What one well-timed power surge could do to Manhattanites at breakfast time?
122 Film sequel about a chauffeur who talks incessantly?
123 Barbecue sites
124 Time gone by
125 Collections

DOWN

1 "Vatican Rag" singer Tom
2 Nervous
3 Zola novel
4 Field Marshal Rommel
5 Article for Helmut
6 Off the job
7 Element in batteries
8 Genus of razor clams
9 Country colleen
10 Not in the book
11 Getting 101 Across
12 Hindu writings
13 Common verb
14 ("Boo-hoo-hoo")
15 Bridge bid
16 Stereo's precursor
17 Fondly remembered Douglas planes
18 *Tres* preceder
19 Tucson campus, familiarly
20 Shortly
22 ___ school
29 Move obliquely
31 My, to Maigret
32 Regular alternative, once
33 Testing room
35 The Bering, for one: abbr.
37 Western Hemisphere alliance: abbr.
39 Tout's concern
40 The same, on the Seine
42 Devastation
43 Actress Verduco
44 Dieter's request
45 The Roscommon people
46 Shoot
47 Naturally followed
48 Goofball
49 Stalwart performers
50 Ruled
54 German pronoun
56 Voice of Daffy
57 Addis ___
61 Frequent flyer, familiarly
62 Hubbub
64 Handle
65 Navel wear?
67 "Friend," to early New England Indians
68 Haitian dance
69 On ___ (busy)
70 Viking in the comics
71 Slangy assent
76 Backtalk
77 Can't stand
78 Turkey
80 Workplace watchdog
81 "Elvira, ___ of the Dark"
82 Stubborn ones
86 "We ___ in our streets" (Lamentations)
88 Bilko, for one: abbr.
89 Deli bread
91 *Evita* role
92 Vietnamese holiday
93 Like crosswords, to fans
98 Release
99 Sirens
100 Erminelike animals
101 "Lustrous ___ of sun" (Walt Whitman)
102 Hard on the ears
103 Chan's creator, Earl ___ Biggers
104 "By ___ was really mad ..."
106 Eager
108 Sno-cones
109 Novelist John Cowper ___
112 Bit or jot
113 Italian TV network
114 A ways away
116 Tim Daly's actress sister
118 Puppy's bite
119 Noted hydroelectric proj.
120 Chant sounds
121 Never, to Nietzsche

ACROSS

1 Whacks a "dog"
6 Plumbing problem
10 Plant equivalent of blood vessels
15 Chew the fat
18 Lie ahead
19 One of Faith's friends?
20 Jack in *Speed*
21 Dispatched car
22 Aerobicised one's doggies?
25 Inveterate
26 Depraved
27 Haul into court
28 Computer organization?
30 0 on an altimeter
34 Forgo play
37 *Passages* author Sheehy
38 Ultimate
39 Fathers
41 Following-suit word
42 Violinist or his actor son
44 ___ the knuckles (like some pitches)
46 Doggie races?
50 Author Gay
52 Collided with
53 Circle area, ___ squared
54 Olive genus
56 Turkey side
57 Frame anew, as a picture
59 Doggie playground?
63 Little Caesar's lead spitter
65 Part of the 78 Across
67 Responsibility
69 Prelude to ahs
70 Two of its counties are Sioux and Custer
71 Fuzz-faced prez
72 Name for a doggie deli?
75 Internal makeup of a sort
76 Kazakhstan follower, once: abbr.
77 Hall of Famer Aparicio
78 Sense of identity
79 Fire, in France
80 Mercury or Saturn
81 Doggie in need of a diet?
84 General's signature
86 Shogun's capital
88 Canal or lake
89 Toy-sized toymaker
91 Comic actor Pendleton
92 Bible book
95 Doggie author?
101 Record spoiler
102 TV exec Arledge
103 Second gardener
104 Tightens, perhaps
106 Game marker
107 Transgressions
108 Ohio team
110 Loreleis
112 Follow
116 Atop, to a scop
118 Grandpa Walton portrayer
119 Debussy subject
120 Ad placed by a footloose doggie?
127 Advantage
128 Whoppers
129 Bee's ward
130 Lasso
131 Attract
132 A bed habit
133 New Jersey team
134 Side building

DOWN

1 Witnessed
2 Rare bill
3 G.A. Nasser's land
4 Entertainer Theodore
5 Martin and Rossi
6 Disease of Asia
7 The Hulk's real first name
8 Chooses
9 Outfit
10 Vintage Jag
11 Slangy affirmative
12 Praise
13 Tied up
14 One of Ataturk's names
15 Island of coffee
16 World War II powers
17 Hard to get around
21 Socialize at a nightclub
23 Find the quotient
24 British P.M., once
29 Is on TV
30 Peeve
31 Ante up?
32 The Pope's doggie?
33 Milk, in Monterrey
35 An appetizer
36 Boom modifier
40 Peres of Israel
43 Photo showing Tormé posing with his doggie?
45 Endowments org.
47 Kiosks
48 Pal, in *A Clockwork Orange* lingo
49 Samantha's lookalike cousin on *Bewitched*
51 Odoriferous
55 Mogul emperor of Hindustan
57 1942 Ginger Rogers film, ___ *Hart*
58 What an eye develops into
60 Husband of Pocahontas
61 Indian butter
62 *Meet the Press* fodder
63 Canadian peninsula
64 Totally involve
66 Ascend
68 Singer portrayed by Jennifer Lopez
73 TV oldie, *You ___ for It*
74 Burning
82 Lamp fuel
83 Playwright Rice
85 Piano piece
87 Globule
90 Best-loved thing, briefly
92 Actress Joanna
93 Othello, for one
94 Erwin and Symington
96 Roulette color
97 Heats glass
98 Soothing
99 Tempted
100 Gets that pins-and-needles feeling
105 Bogart film, *High ___*
109 Attach, as buttons
111 Actress Jeanne
112 Some
113 Board groove
114 Science fiction award
115 Eye
117 Ready to eat
121 Burnt sienna, for one
122 Cleopatra's fatal friend
123 English subj.
124 It'll move you
125 Paris when it sizzles
126 Too easygoing

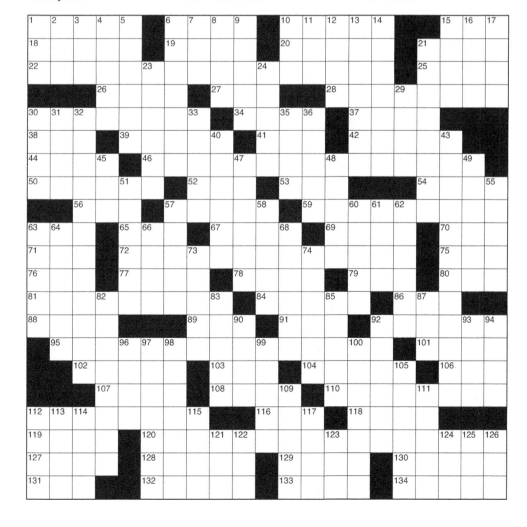

46 Fashion Your Seat Belts

...Someone's putting you on

ACROSS

1 Bad report card
5 Home of swallows?
11 English horn cousin
15 Shoot the breeze
19 Scatter's first name
20 Brand name for a versatile fashion?
22 Flavor from the garden
23 Being a student of fashion?
25 Stick-figure smiles
26 IRS personified
27 Scotch diluter
28 Ideologue's drama
30 Egyptian goddess
33 Singer Sumac
35 Amazonian with amps
36 One in Father Damien's care
40 Fitting room taboo?
47 Ice maneuver
48 Craze
49 *The Joy Luck Club* author
50 Boring event
52 Undress?
56 Routing word
57 City council enactment: abbr.
58 Erwin and others
59 Bath beverage
60 No fewer than
64 High spars
67 Farewell piece
70 Squealer
71 Fashion-shop smoking rule?
75 Work with
76 Vintage cars
77 Sheet fabrics
79 Tree-lined walk
83 August sign
85 People pieces, briefly
86 Provence preposition
88 January slowpoke
89 Trendy boutique specializing in ensembles?
94 Phone attachment?
97 Chorus syllable
98 Daytime fare
99 Japanese VIP of WWII
100 Slipping into something comfortable?
104 Post-joke query
105 Revival prefix
106 "Pay" addition
107 Small amount
109 Salads with salsa
114 Saluted symbol
117 Bill's predecessor
122 Poker stake
123 Shop frequented by organ grinders?
127 Ahab's mark
128 Shop specializing in parkas?
129 NFL team
130 Isles hit by Georges
131 Fleming villain
132 Honda rival
133 Plus

DOWN

1 Fedora fabric
2 Shih Tzu invader
3 Linen source
4 Where cotton comes from, e.g.
5 Abby and Ann
6 Bird with a house
7 Joplin piece
8 Leftovers
9 Seuss's *Horton Hears* ___
10 1960s T-shirt style
11 Finder's cry
12 Rum cake
13 First name of fashion
14 Famed cow and others
15 1992 Robert Downey Jr. role
16 Munich Mr.
17 Chevron rival
18 Cough syrup amt.
21 Piccadilly vehicles
24 Not Neet?
29 Dick Tracy's wife
31 Pressed for time
32 Tunesmith
34 Re
36 Composer Schifrin
37 Work hard
38 Vet
39 TV Tarzan
41 A day in Durango
42 ___ avis
43 A dog's dog
44 Czarina of the 1700s
45 Science show
46 Mix of *blanc et noir*
48 Changed, in a way
51 Enjoy a potlatch
53 Absorb effortlessly
54 Shirts next to skirts
55 It gets owed fast
61 Underwear fabrics
62 Ancient Sumerian city (or a big dent in a Peugeot?)
63 Latin abbr.
65 Jack Horner's prize
66 Compass pt.
68 Data to be entered: abbr.
69 Safeguard against overstepping, in the shot-put
72 Run for it
73 Curling-iron user, e.g.
74 Fashionable and then some
78 Conductor Ozawa
79 Boon to alfresco banking, familiarly
80 Secular
81 Suffix meaning "ruler"
82 Italian wine center
84 Crosby film, *The Bells* ___ *Mary's*
87 Jam
90 Great pot?
91 Bard baddie
92 *Monarque*
93 Sunny *saison*
95 Haranguers-on
96 Old draft status
101 *Breathless* director
102 Actress Woodard
103 Superior ability
104 Hoover and Tolson
108 Where Aesop shopped
109 Something to do
110 *The* ___ *and Future King*
111 Order to Benji
112 On ___ (very similar)
113 Play *Wheel of Fortune*
115 Motet part
116 Pass, as time
118 New Orleans vegie
119 Not plastic
120 Places to play indoors
121 Exxon, before
124 Latin lover's word
125 Back again
126 A Rocky foe

ACROSS

1 Thinking aids?
5 Crosby, Stills & ___
9 Parts of a washboard stomach, briefly
12 It goes with the airflow
16 Grab bag
17 Popular cookie
18 Bed crosspiece
19 Alfred the Great was one
20 Single-channel syst.
21 A ___ TIP (apt anagram of "pittance")
22 Author of *Honor Thy Yakking Father*?
24 Graffiti from a certain *Flintstones* fan?
27 Bolivian bear
28 ___ roll
29 Juice points under the hood
30 Subside
33 Symbolic slander
34 Sicilian peak
35 Baseball's Kaline and others
36 Vermilion
38 Title for a woman who's a light eater?
45 Location
46 Exploiting
47 Start of many Southwestern cities

48 Don't work
49 Comical Catherine
50 "___ soak your head!"
51 See 47 Across
52 What the sot started doing?
55 Go through an infant stage
57 Skater's finale, often
59 Has ___ pot
60 Airport abbr.
61 A Gabor
63 You stay here
65 Ursula Andress film
66 Instance, in France
69 Magician's word
71 Composer Charles
73 Ideally
75 Fat bird's walk?
79 Focus of a driving obsession
81 Choir member
82 ___ as Methuselah
83 Heyerdahl's second papyrus boat
84 "Feels good" sound
85 Deck view
86 Rapids transit
87 Noel Coward song about loving a man in uniform?
91 Mowgli's python friend
92 Pep rally site
93 Plunder

94 Over there, back then
95 Jenny of weight loss
97 Honchos in headdresses
100 "___-lish!"
101 Cyclamate banner: abbr.
104 What frustrated solvers may end up doing today?
108 Once-popular kids' cereal in Brazil?
111 Anise-flavored aperitif
112 *Inter* ___
113 **CrOW**ds
114 Leftovers
115 Fishing spot
116 PED act
117 Pivot point
118 Priest's add-on
119 Apt author of *The Never-Ending Story*
120 Ox attachment

DOWN

1 Jazz quartet, e.g.
2 Fugard's *A Lesson from* ___
3 Bean or car
4 Chimney coating
5 Slangy "sorry"
6 Don King booking
7 Fax
8 Relaxing soaks
9 *Tiny Alice* playwright
10 ___ breath (flower)

11 With poly and 15 Down, a plastic
12 Curbside employee
13 Rail splitter
14 ZIP Codes, for ex.
15 See 11 Down
18 Shore floor
19 Bargain events
22 Express dissatisfaction
23 Veil material
25 Acting Gig
26 Novelist Rice
31 Heep of trouble
32 It means "rock"
33 "... she loves ___ ..."
34 Some collars
35 Funny lyricist Sherman and others
37 Situation
38 Proportion
39 The Poe House
40 *The* ___ *Sanction*
41 EPCOT's st.
42 "___ were you ..."
43 Kin of a bauble
44 Nickname of basketball great Oscar Robertson
45 Chasing word
49 Eightsome
51 Vegas roll
52 1992 Earth Summit city
53 "___ we meet again"
54 *The Merry Widow* composer
56 Salome's wish granter
58 Triskaideka follower
62 Hindu retreat
64 She had an Arden following
66 Glitterati member
67 Take ___ at (try)
68 Rife with rock
69 Bombard
70 Insect-loving leaper
72 Great guy?
74 Breakfast option
75 Central, for one
76 Stern with a bow
77 Really succeed
78 Drop cloth?
80 "Feels good" sound
84 Stick it in your ear
85 Some woodwinds
87 Mary Wells classic
88 Cassini et al.
89 Tucson school, to locals
90 Trash-strewn lot, e.g.
92 Young female pigs
96 Fatty ___
97 People with handles
98 Sword parts
99 Dom Pedro's ill-fated wife
100 Drifted (off)
101 Big sheet
102 Swig
103 Aphorism
105 Elks' letters
106 Drive to bankruptcy, maybe
107 Ceraceous
108 Housing agcy.
109 Reviewer Reed
110 Swiss canton

ACROSS

1 Mr. Z of Hollywood
6 South Seas souvenir
9 Low, low opera voice
14 FDR's dog
18 Shopping area next to the Camel Lot?
20 Attorney, at times
21 "___ written ..."
22 Mask shop inventory?
23 Ugly Stepsister's problem?
25 Ripening agent
26 Hair care products
28 Stretch inning
29 Lola in *Damn Yankees*
31 Production construction
33 Buster Brown's dog
34 Homer's H
35 Blueprint details: abbr.
38 Ingrid, in *Casablanca*
40 Song of celebration sung by Noah?
43 Without shame
45 Life in France?
47 ___ bad time
48 Letters on some Indy cars
49 Emulated Petruchio
50 1985 film with a Neanderthal sense of humor
52 Deputy or A.D.C.
56 "___ or just no good?" (Geraldo segment about Adam and Eve?)
59 Actress Rigg
60 War zone of January 1991
61 TV's Maude or Dorothy
62 ___ of society (Lot's wife, perhaps)
64 Reagan's Star Wars prog.
66 Out-of-it kitties?
70 Quarters with a no.
71 Go for the gold
73 The downbeat is usually on it
74 Act like a Hun
76 Gray ___
77 Flan critic's outburst?
83 Cheeks describer
84 Deletes
85 Old German coin
86 Teddy, to John Jr.
89 Captain Kirk's successor, Jean-___ Picard
90 Screw up
91 Act like Lisa, not Bart
92 Warning sign at a porcupine farm?
97 Stomping grounds: abbr.
99 Compass dir.
100 Surprised cries
101 Actor Carroll
102 Actress Joanne
103 Actress Bonet
105 Sells (for)
107 Editorialized
110 Assignment
114 "The ___" (bathroom edition of *Silas Marner*, etc.?)
118 Proselytize on the islands?
120 1963 role for Shirley
121 A real pain in the ear
122 Nickname for a crook who's easy to track?
123 Gimlet or goggle follower
124 A dynamite personality
125 Zuider ___
126 Irritable partner?

DOWN

1 Salmon tail?
2 Something to wave
3 Give rankings to
4 Reason to call 911: abbr.
5 Utmost, briefly
6 Romance language speakers
7 Classic Lotus sports car model
8 Homelessness, drug abuse, etc.
9 Cousin of "mac"
10 In the past
11 Wd. ending
12 Vietnam's region: abbr.
13 Daniel and Humberto
14 Marching-band flute
15 Very sorry individual
16 Ray of *GoodFellas*
17 "And strange ___ may sound ..."
19 Just
20 On a caravel
24 Head off
27 Respect
30 Kiangs and onagers
32 Recruit
33 Sung syllables
35 Mil. class on campus
36 Movie-rating org.
37 Nickels?
39 Lemmon film set in Italy
41 Of a heart part
42 "... fetch ___ of water"
44 Hawaiian goose
46 Pianist Pogorelich
50 Cured with salt
51 Talk-a-thon
53 Hamlet's comment at dinner?
54 Hiking of a football
55 Like lemon meringue
57 Intersect
58 "You ___ like a man!" (Vito Corleone)
59 Major quakes, e.g.
63 Bolívar liberated it
64 Mark of the vampire?
65 Stella of cookie fame
67 Fill
68 Acted like Lorelei
69 "You've cut me to the quick!"
72 Come across with the dough
75 Salty state
78 Record again, captain-style
79 Exhausts
80 I or II Bible bk.
81 Guns the engine
82 Attracted
87 The truth
88 Used, as a prayer rug
91 Type of shower
92 Bombing raid
93 The Big Bang, for one
94 27 Down, to a *mademoiselle*
95 Keep one's ___ the grindstone
96 Fox steps?
98 Mournful *poeme*
104 "Thereby hangs ___"
106 "When I was ___ ..."
108 Don Juan's mom
109 Tag info
111 One mo' time
112 Nunn and Spade
113 Banjo's resting place
115 Freedom of mvmt.?
116 Resident's ending
117 Cruet contents
119 Calif. time

ACROSS

1 Sunset, for one
6 Boaters and bowlers
10 Actress Dawber
13 Luminous ring
14 Ore veins
15 Frank's second wife
16 *?*
18 Word after United or American
19 Like the taste of some toothpastes
20 Ashton Tate computer software
21 "Out of" opposite
22 It was Freud's idea
23 Explorer Leif
25 "___ as I can figure ..."
27 *?*
30 Kin of a mania
31 Agreement
33 "Self" starter?
34 The summer ___ (on or about June 21)
38 Lawyers' org.
39 Japanese wrestling
40 *?*
42 "Certainly"
43 Golfers' grp.
44 Took a pew
45 Liquid butter of India
46 1960s dancing
49 *?*
52 Coat infesters
53 Alabama rival
56 "You're locked ___ with no windows or doors ..." (start of many a mystery puzzle)
57 Ultimatum words
58 Famed D.C. bookstore, Politics & ___
59 *?*
61 Knight's contest
62 Nothin' special
64 Ms. Richards of Texas
65 Fall mo.
66 Low point
69 *?*
72 Favorable votes
73 Neither follower
74 Newspaper for bright people?
75 Melville opus
76 Pre-1917 ruler
77 County N of San Francisco
79 *?*
82 Secure again, as a door
83 Luis on *Sesame Street*, Emilio ___ (anagram of OLD-AGED)
85 Shade tree
86 On
87 Mr. Root or Mr. Yale
88 Maker of Macs
90 Name for the devil
91 *?*
95 Buck's mate
96 Knight-time protection
97 Singer Sheena
98 Time line features: abbr.
99 "That's agreeable"
100 Kentucky Derby flowers

DOWN

1 Do a tedious post office job
2 Supper supporter
3 Sitter on *le trône*
4 Pilgrim's stop
5 Englander's ending for encyclo
6 "In what way?"
7 Sell mates?
8 It's steeped in tradition
9 I.D. often needed on invoices: abbr.
10 Indian who's always in hock?
11 Embodiment
12 La Guardia was one
13 Indian craft
14 A new ___ life
16 Lower in fat or calories
17 *?*
19 Paradises, of a sort
21 Deceiver
23 With "plasm," seance stuff
24 Greek letter
25 Like a house ___
26 The Mennonites, e.g.
28 Robert of *The Man from U.N.C.L.E.*
29 Resident of a west Arizona city
31 Fork over
32 Reconstruction guy
35 Cartoon rooster, Foghorn ___
36 East Indian evergreen (anagram of MISCHA)
37 Elect. day
39 Seed, of a sort
40 Akbar the Great, ___-ud-Din Muhammad
41 Christmas song
44 Older folks
47 Heating fuel
48 Sugar ending
49 ___ in the bucket
50 Montana's nickname
51 ___-so (what's-his-name)
52 Worries
53 Likely
54 Infamous Geller
55 Cheeky
57 ___ twice (seldom)
60 Old TV game show, *Who ___ Trust?*
62 Simon Templar, the ___
63 Stringbean Olive
66 Contact-cleaner ingredient
67 Jungle snake
68 "Baby, it's co-o-old outside"
70 Get exactly right
71 To forget, to Guy Forget
72 Bullets, etc.
75 Last word in the pease porridge rhyme
76 Phones
77 Sky streaker
78 Igloos and yurts
80 Actor Harry of *Tales of the Texas Rangers* (anagram of U R LATE)
81 Fasten again
82 Quaid or Travis
83 Prefix meaning "skin"
84 Young Jetson
88 Johnson of *Laugh-In*
89 What some cons are
91 Investigative arm of Congress: abbr.
92 Noah's vessel
93 Chairman, once
94 CIA predecessor

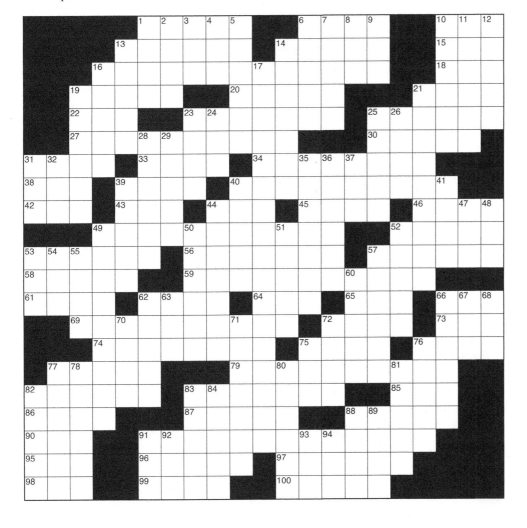

ACROSS

1 Hydrogen ___ (gas that smells like rotten eggs)
8 Flop
12 Florence sits on it
16 Something to stand on
19 Beaver's last name
20 Soprano's neighbor
21 Turn sharply
22 Resident of San Simian?
23 Cup-shaped flower
24 Interrupted film about Southern farmers?
27 Military or music abbr.
28 Made tracks
29 Pianist Rudolf
30 Whitman's dooryard bloomers
31 Half-wild, half-domesticated canine
34 Gide's good
35 Conceal
36 A step ahead of the MPs
38 Interrupted blue-collar spinoff of *Dallas*?
45 Rise up
47 Darned spot
48 Barrister's quaff
49 Mr. Kazan
50 Laid orbs on
51 Interrupted aerobics-show theme?
57 Photographer Adams
58 Oligocene critters (literally, "toothed mountain dwellers")
60 Last gasps for gamblers
61 Plutocrat's digs
62 Mount that Moses climbed
63 Recommended amt.
64 Dew Drop and Dolly Wright
65 Canadian prov.
66 Sinking signal
67 Interrupted show about prune-loving private eyes?
72 Detour abbr.
75 "You betcha"
76 Letterman's time
77 Hawaiian tuna
78 Supermodel who wed David Bowie in 1992
82 Awakened, in a way
84 Bust bottom
85 Frankenstein neck feature
87 Jannings and Gilels
88 With 96 Across, the other Tammany Hall scandal?
90 "Too much!"
91 Opposite of *sud*
92 Golfer Hogan
93 Auction gesture
94 Ark of the Covenant, e.g.
96 See 88 Across
103 Oft-dedicated poetry
104 ___-Contra
105 Jousting title?
106 Muscadet wine city
108 A Musketeer
111 Take to a higher authority
114 Sizable: abbr.
115 Geometry proof abbr.
118 Interrupted series about a cramped flying saucer?
120 Blend
122 Parent co. of Universal Pictures
123 Glass coloration
124 Anarchist Goldman
125 Hop on an iron horse
126 Astronomer's tableau
127 "Wine-dark" places
128 Some grains
129 Lives

DOWN

1 Bait-and-switch, e.g.
2 Arm bone
3 Interrupted actor who'd been sitting around too long anyway?
4 Clan: abbr.
5 A paler shade of white
6 Don't mention it, in Durango
7 Previously, to the Bard
8 Diet restrictions
9 Skin cream herb
10 Pianist José
11 Attach firmly
12 Mary Kay rival
13 Boxer separator
14 Starting-over goal
15 Maker of Tater Tots
16 Aa or pahoehoe
17 *Roots* was one
18 Hair goos
25 Guesser's plea
26 Tin is one
32 Ring cheer
33 Bask successfully
35 A living nightmare
36 Incendiary crime
37 "___ not amused"
39 Heaps
40 Luau accessory
41 Linden and Roach
42 *Casablanca* role and namesakes
43 Mislead intentionally
44 Elihu and Linus
46 '60s mindbender
52 Go downhill
53 Settle
54 "A big fat hen" preceder
55 Recipient
56 Unseat
57 Italian wine city
59 JFK's spy hero
61 Caruso or Fermi
64 ___ *Teen-age Werewolf*
65 Last box on a questionnaire
68 Mirror-breaker's bad-luck span, briefly
69 A concrete amount
70 Crusades crusher
71 Part of a circle's area
72 Demetrius's workplace
73 Slot machine fruit
74 Classic Ford, familiarly
79 Interrupted show about lawn-care crimefighters?
80 ___ of one's own medicine
81 Salamanders
83 "That ___ religion"
84 See 59 Down
85 Sierra Club sci.
86 Baby's need, for short
88 Word in a Joe McCarthy question
89 Biol. blueprint
92 Pet
95 Weed yanker
97 Watch sites
98 Some snakes
99 Dog in old RCA logos
100 Gorgeous, to a girl
101 More subdued
102 V-8, for one
107 *Gray's Anatomy* et al.
108 Baksheesh
109 Top 40 format
110 Fired, as a torpedo
111 Mound dwellers
112 Pinnacle
113 Poetic pastures
116 City or canal
117 Hibernation stations
119 ___ big way
121 Angle or cycle preceder

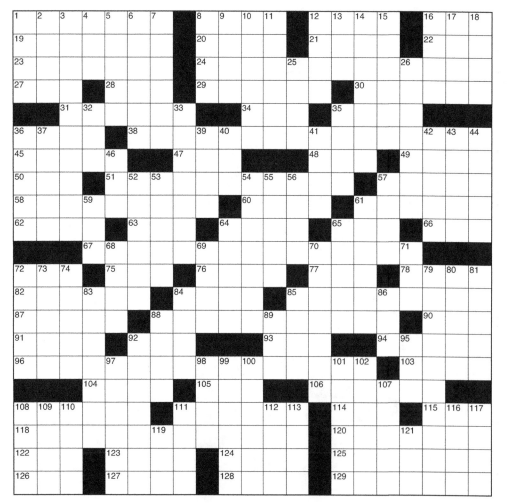

New England-Style Chatter 2

...Or Kennedy 101

ACROSS

1 Precarious perch
5 Coffee coast
9 Made crow sounds
14 Heart problem?
18 Where the ounce can pounce
19 A No. 2, on the green
20 Veteran
21 Old mother Hubbard's son
22 Huck Finn parodies?
24 Bordello special?
26 Filch a la Poe
27 Science org.
29 R-V center?
30 William who wed Mary
31 Verb in "I Am Woman"
32 Perennial phone problem at Goats R Us?
37 Your, in Tours
39 Fly catcher of a sort
40 ___ double take
41 "___ a date!"
42 Actress who felt empty inside?
46 Rival whisky of Old Argyle?
51 Guy's name or French word
52 Have a rough night
53 Deck a Dolphin
55 Rex Reed rejection
56 Family of fancy birds
58 Written twice, a dance
59 Distaff reference
62 Language ending
63 Idaho staple
64 Moon jumper
66 Battled Cochise?
69 "___ drunkard" (Rick, in *Casablanca*)
71 Shortened, as a dict.
73 Capt. of industry
74 Butt heads
75 Sun-roof safeguard on some U.S. cars?
80 *Vanity Fair* author's monogram
82 *Iliad* suicide
86 Old undercover org.
87 Bristol break
88 Actor Tognazzi
89 1987 Coppola film, *Gardens ___*
91 Place with good circulation?
92 Uses, as a futon
95 Lovable eccentric
96 Sit or shut endings
97 Rollers in barracks?
101 One-time Miracle Gro pitchman?
104 Certain pol: abbr.
105 Meadow
107 Corn-eater's leftover
108 *Lover Come Back* star
109 What a nail feels?
115 Car-collecting comedian
118 Pal, to Pascal
119 *Cinco de mayo*, e.g.
120 Inning enders
121 Go along with Marie Antoinette
124 With 128 Across, good advice at the Medicine Man Ball?
128 See 124 Across
130 African Nobelist
131 U.K. hotspot
132 Who-knows-how-long
133 Bank take-back
134 African antelope
135 European steel center
136 Others
137 Goddess of discord

DOWN

1 Reading aid
2 "Peace ___ profession" (*Dr. Strangelove* sign)
3 Film or phone preceder
4 Turkish treat
5 New Zealander
6 Shaggy ape, briefly
7 The best, briefly
8 Poe's Lee
9 Store sign
10 Commotion
11 Typist's stat: abbr.
12 Edit, sometimes
13 "___ under the apple tree ..."
14 Tirana's land: abbr.
15 Stevens or T. Nelson
16 Mandel or Morris
17 "The ___ near ..."
20 Spoken
23 1992 World Series champs
25 Singer Springfield
28 Chief monk
33 Rice U. team
34 Penalized amount
35 Paw
36 Animal you can sit on
38 Display to good advantage
42 Cherokee, for one
43 Son of Rebecca
44 Capital on a fjord
45 Baylor University's city
47 Binet-Simon, for one
48 Crude org.
49 Express-lane requirement, often
50 Bended part
51 Previous records?
54 Cut of beef
57 Nest-egg guarantor: abbr.
60 Insurance city
61 Ecol.-minded entity
65 Route
66 Pre-osculated princes
67 Start of many questions
68 Latin verb
70 Grocery store: abbr.
72 "... devil and the deep ___"
75 Pear variety
76 Stamp ctr.
77 ___ large (hasn't been caught)
78 Cabbage or moolah
79 Not too receptive
81 Early keyboard synthesizer
83 Enlist in
84 Dustin's *Graduate* costar
85 Illiterate John Hancocks
90 Black bomber
93 *Winnie ___ Pu*
94 Sleep time, in Stuttgart
95 Market-watching cable channel
98 *Of Human Bondage* author's initials
99 Takes to heart
100 Henry, in Hermosillo
102 Ohio college town
103 Vision supervision
106 12
109 "It ___ Be You"
110 Love in Paris
111 Like a julep
112 Bank-job scores
113 Litigant
114 Sharpens
116 Title giver
117 Giraffe's cousin
122 Della, to Perry: abbr.
123 Early grandson, in the Bible
125 Rented outfit
126 Man of Steel emblem
127 Summer, in Lyon
129 Mortar mixer

52 Food Naming: A Report Card ...Care for an unappetizer?

ACROSS

1 Tope opener
4 Make ___ (complain)
9 My gal
12 Spurious name
17 Mo. of decision
18 Recipient
19 "___ boy!"
20 WWII field marshal, familiarly
21 Popular bread spread (grade: F)
23 Another popular bread spread (grade: F)
25 Powder or shoe follower
26 "Mighty ___ a Rose"
27 English hymnologist John Mason ___
28 Myrmecology specimen
29 Picture taker, briefly
31 Deli purchase (grade: F)
36 Popular chocolate/nut candies (grade: F)
39 A direction, in Durango
40 ___ kleine Nachtmusik
41 Tristan's love
42 Collectibles ending
43 Type of dive or song
45 Pretend
46 Meat entree (grade: F)
53 Cobb and Hardin
54 Hospital battery
56 Casablanca's Lund et al.
57 Teachers' org.
58 Polite term of address
59 Rose supporters
60 Destroyer detector
62 Meat entree (grade: F)
67 Indian corn
68 Has a taste for
69 Busby Berkeley's real name
70 Raw resource
71 Let in or let on
72 Pop
74 Picture tube: abbr.
77 Chinese appetizer (grade: F)
81 One with a rash or a yen
83 411 respondent: abbr.
84 Bi plus 1
85 ___ on (get drunk)
86 Tampa Bay talk-radio station (or its location in the state)
88 Cowboy humorist's full name, William Penn ___ Rogers
91 Breakfast cereal (grade: F)
92 Betty Crocker side dish (grade: F)
96 You, politely, in German
97 Well goo
98 Insurance giant
99 The little guy
101 Sky bear
104 Bakery items (grade: F)
107 Dessert (grade: F)
109 Forget-___
110 QED section
111 Places
112 Promise to pay
113 Cookies
114 "Send help"
115 Ex-Chicago mayor Jane
116 She's coming out

DOWN

1 Short distance
2 Area near TriBeCa
3 Stays on the range too long?
4 Cutting tool
5 Ducks, geese, and turkeys
6 Takes off one's cloche
7 Japanese watchmaker
8 States, in comix
9 Mason's secretary
10 Order to relax
11 Eric Clapton classic
12 I love, in Latin
13 Coach Holtz
14 Doubled up, perhaps
15 Immediately
16 Elect. keyboard
19 ___ dei
22 Empower
24 Pig's digs
30 Do zen
32 Taboo list
33 Paraphernalia
34 Honeybunch
35 Grape abuser
36 With "free," a common redundancy
37 Anthem start
38 Damage the patched spot
42 Quick
43 One who puts things away
44 Grains and karats: abbr.
47 Flying ttoys
48 Extorted
49 Gomer's org.
50 Jo or Rose follower
51 Madonna's ex
52 Prepare to feather
55 Suppress anger, e.g.
58 Les ___
59 Undoes an edit
60 Dundee dogs
61 Assents
62 Lucknow attire
63 Wharf extension
64 Intentions
65 Burnett vignette
66 Latin phrase of position
67 Often angry assemblage
71 Fuel suffix
72 Grand Canyon transit
73 A wire service
74 Of an ancient illness
75 Actor Santoni
76 Fierce dinosaur, in shorthand
78 Big grower in Hawaii
79 Resorts of sorts
80 Of the ear
82 Element in photoelectric cells
86 Paler
87 Socks or Stimpy
88 Conductor Toscanini
89 Douglas and Reed
90 "And ___ of thousands"
91 Funny Dennis or Larry
92 Mag that "exposed" Burt
93 Cheer, of a sort
94 Neuwirth and Rebozo
95 Suspicious
100 Mexican dessert
102 Plumlike fruit
103 Rub follow-up
105 Dove sound
106 Chess pcs.
107 Boxer's blow
108 Sugar ending

53 Bed and Breakfast Alternatives

...A little this and that

ACROSS

1 *Murder, She Wrote* network
4 Delighted cries
7 Unoriginal
11 Holding tanks, in a way
17 Small branching, of a sort
19 Dave Garroway's signoff
20 Supernatural
21 "Did ___ the one about ..."
22 Spectacle pioneers
24 Basic
26 Director Howard
27 Some salmon
28 Wall St. hotshot
29 Pyrite, e.g.
30 Whistle-wetter in Watford
32 "___ in 'Tom'"
34 Fred's neighbors, on TV
40 A pair, in Paisley
42 Bounce on one's knee
45 Oogenesis subjects
46 Govt. check issuer
47 Where the rubber meets the road
49 Hartford foe
51 High-tech East Coast sch.
52 Paul Scott's "The ___ Quartet"
55 Old college cheer
56 23rd Psalm verb
57 Livid
62 ___ corpus
64 Reminiscer's word
65 Help out on the hwy.
66 Show shock
68 Poet's word
69 No-more-seats sign
70 Carl said he never said it
75 Typical guy's exclamation?
76 ___ *supra*
77 Adjutant, e.g.
78 Director Grosbard
79 Counterpart of dim., in music
80 Spent
83 Sexy subject
88 Race for Alain Prost
90 With 4 Down, whose cow?
92 ___ handstand
93 Actress Merkel
94 Champaign's sister
95 Sees or sites
97 Adjusted opening?
100 Altercation
101 Actress Patricia
102 Actress Peeples
104 1948 Oscar tune
108 Little marvel
110 Rejuvenation station
112 Night, in Glasgow
113 British verb ending
114 Like Alistair Cooke: abbr.
116 Immigrants take it: abbr.
118 Classy movie duo
124 Personal assets
127 Dressing choice
129 Crime-world go-between
130 Brings home
131 Dogfight participant
132 Underpriced items
133 Grant and March
134 Kristi Yamaguchi's surface
135 Magazine famous for its fold-in

DOWN

1 ___ wolf
2 Bumbler
3 Old, as milk
4 See 90 Across
5 Hair restraints
6 Maroon
7 The cop in *It's A Wonderful Life*
8 Kent's love
9 Integra maker
10 Dress line
11 Gray wolf
12 Quitter's motto
13 AT&T rival
14 Market types
15 Shoo-fly pie ingredient
16 Charon's river
18 Stage: abbr.
19 Invention protection
22 Kukla's creator
23 Florida wrecker of 1992
25 Lethal wrapper
31 British inc.
33 Gulf E of Djibouti
34 Turkey
35 Old Nick's thing
36 "So long"
37 Wire cutter?
38 Stumble
39 Slangy OK
41 Abe Lincoln's sign
43 Cast off inhibitions
44 Callback?
48 Climactic cry
50 Young ___ (kids)
53 Pertaining to pond scum
54 Evita's guy
56 It's covered with film
58 Fratricidal guy
59 Baseball's Daniels
60 Buñuel-Dali film of 1929, *An ___ Dog*
61 Double curve
63 Ravel work
67 Ling-Ling was one
69 Cold shoulder
70 Completely, colloquially
71 Wild goat
72 Lobster catcher?
73 "Look what ___!"
74 Chan portrayer Warner
75 Diving bird
79 "Son of" sequel?
80 Museum piece
81 Out caller
82 Math homewk.
84 Butler's last word, 1939
85 Disneyland prefix
86 Sufficient, old-style
87 Aphorisms
89 Ghostlike
91 Chef Potts?
95 Sucker
96 Ben and Gertrude
98 Of a continent
99 Design a garden
103 Easter is one
105 Kite's props
106 ___ off (intermittently)
107 Ultimate, in a way
109 Detector's find
111 James Garfield's middle name
114 Slips (away)
115 In apple-pie order
117 Thes. entries
119 Resembling paddles
120 Wins, in a card game
121 Actress Andersson
122 Actor Neeson
123 Actress Turner
125 Actress Thurman
126 Actress Arthur
128 Actor Beatty

54 Trick Question

...It's criminal what passes for humor these days

ACROSS

1 The answer I was expecting to the riddle in this puzzle
7 Jabber
10 A card game, not a singing style
14 Jokers
18 They have mysterious odas
19 Get-together, of a sort
21 Remote refuge
22 Like bedroom eyes
23 **Start of a riddle**
25 Easy multiplier
26 Creepy creatures
28 Boyfriend
29 Start of a verse?
30 TV colleague of Goldie and Lily
31 The lessor amount
33 Sounds like a bomb
35 With 10 Down, a dead end
38 **Riddle, part 2**
43 Mimicked
44 Minor worker
45 Need replacing
46 **Riddle, part 3**
50 The "come back" kid
51 Penultimate letter
54 "... my soul ___"
55 Yvonne's evening
57 Galileo and Garibaldi
59 Caution sign
61 City 155 miles SE of San Francisco
63 Discarded metal
64 Knockout props
67 **Riddle, part 4**
70 Pacing, perhaps
71 Gave the eye to
73 City near Cleveland
74 Blimp, e.g.
76 "It never ___ amaze me"
78 *Murder, She Wrote* doctor
80 Where peas live
84 Essential
85 Carpenter's spinner
87 **Riddle, part 5**
89 Estate dividers
91 Bemused remark
92 "It's ___ big mistake!"
93 **Riddle, part 6**
98 Most of the earth's surface
99 Frasier's brother
100 Pelvis parts
101 Time out?
103 ___ for effort
104 Connecticut Ivy Leaguers
108 Rifleman Lucas and son Mark
110 B. Favre and S. Young, once

113 **End of the riddle**
116 Prof's security
118 Part of the country
119 Little links
120 *The Night of the ___*
121 Frosty's freaky cousin?
122 Where the sidewalk meets the road, in Britain
123 Tokyo, once
124 The answer I wasn't expecting to the riddle in this puzzle

DOWN

1 David's 1960s deskmate
2 Unusually good
3 Whacker for Faldo
4 Rendezvoused
5 Political refugee
6 Tie or track
7 Southerner's boat?
8 "Cotton Candy" blower
9 Any of a well-known nine
10 See 35 Across
11 Push-button alternative
12 Archetypal American co.
13 Melodic subject, in music
14 Convince (with "over")
15 In itself
16 Russian opera composer
17 Defining "carriers" as "mailmen," perhaps
20 Commercial claim!
24 Whips with a pistol?
27 Freezing-temperature word
30 221-B Baker et al.
32 Square root of *nueve*
34 Communications giant: abbr.
35 Players
36 At the level of
37 Pipe gripe
39 Sponsorship
40 Hawaiian girl
41 Serious speakers
42 Barrett or Jaffe
44 Slangy $100 bill
47 Part of 34 Down
48 *Volare*
49 Employers
51 Pal o' mine on a palomino
52 Catch
53 1960s series with a Culp following
56 Does again, as a bow
58 Skating arena
60 Stimulated
62 Prefix meaning "standing"
64 Punch
65 Author-critic James
66 Word after word or sword
68 A word for God
69 Reprove mildly
72 Dispatched nits
75 Clinton and Gore after November 1992
77 "That's ___ there is, there ain't no Mort" (Herb Caen)
79 The H of W.H. Auden
81 Ton o' dough
82 Enid's home: abbr.
83 Grand old man
86 "Once ___ die"
88 "___ say more?"
89 Runner Sebastian
90 Major Idaho river
93 Sort of
94 Cassiterite
95 Red Bordeaux
96 Kidman or Miller
97 Added (on) as an afterthought
98 Lake in James Fenimore Cooper stories
102 Mischievous
105 Sure thing, in sports
106 "___ hollers ..."
107 *The Lion King* villain
109 In the matter of
110 University green
111 Part of "Bren," the gun
112 Line of clothing?
114 My ___, Vietnam
115 Type of bone or joint?
117 Role for Whoopi, 1992 and 1993

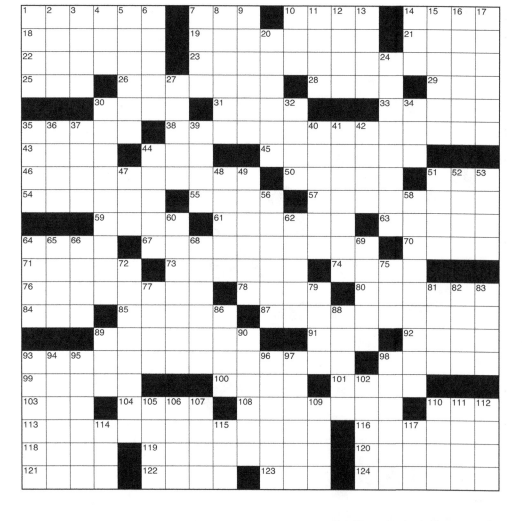

ACROSS

1 T.E. Lawrence portrayer
7 Towns built on springs
11 Lass
17 Appeared to approve
18 Nut from Louisiana
20 Singer who appeared in *The Godfather*
21 *Mister Ed* star
22 Odd-numbered page
23 Adheres to the rules
24 Stump-removal need, sometimes
25 Man of La Mancha?
27 Impatient
29 Meat stamp letters
30 Tackles cacography
33 Christmas tree
35 Alleged babe of Abe
37 Passes over
39 Impede, variantly
40 Crossword WASP (white Anglo-Saxon peon)
42 Keep from having
45 Hawaii's coffee coast
47 The end of 24 Across as we know it?
48 1970s First Lady
49 Bob's partner, in boxing
51 Where Californians get their culture?
54 James Brown's "hot" former backup band
56 Whereabouts: abbr.
57 Ossuaries
58 *Courage Under Fire*'s Ryan
59 McNally books
60 Broken mirror, for example
62 Little spasm
63 ___ grievance (complain officially)
65 The ultimate ending
66 Peke, for one
68 Wins
71 It means "horse"
75 Dracula's inspiration
77 Sandwich shops
78 Friend
80 Trite
81 Blossomed, e.g.
84 Twaddle
85 Eat at Joseph's
86 "A ___ on you!"
87 Major crime
89 Cy Young-winning pitcher of 1968 and 1969
92 Carriage or Martin
93 20 Across and others
94 Aegean island
95 Gratingly off-key
96 PC system
97 Hefty, hefty, hefty
99 Lunch time, roughly
101 Pan's land
104 "My man"
105 Does a tiring job?
108 Throat-peering request
110 Baseball family name
113 Eccentric
115 Some of the succotash
117 Secret identity?
118 Beatles hit of 1967
120 Mixing-bowl instruction
122 It has two spears and a shield on a black, red, and green background
125 Barnstormed, e.g.
126 Jeweler's magnifier
127 Anon
128 Actress Laura
129 It's more, to some
130 Lechers and butterflies

DOWN

1 EPCOT's environs
2 Uke player Herbert Khaury
3 Mrs. Lennon
4 Spanish abbr. of a well-known peace org.
5 126 Across, e.g.
6 Trimmed
7 Tuft producers
8 Aase's son
9 Assisted (by), as a pianist: abbr.
10 Please
11 Person in a proa
12 End of custom?
13 "I'm enjoying myself immensely"
14 "*Buenas ___*"
15 Writer Bagnold
16 Writer Ephron
17 Slalom opening
19 Response to the Little Red Hen
20 Speed abbr.
26 Directory info: abbr.
28 Very best
31 Polynesian amulet
32 Unfeeling
34 Hobbled
36 Bulletin
38 It smells on a pig
41 Greek portico
42 Margot Fonteyn's title
43 Bet. 6 and 10 p.m.
44 Funny Louis et al.
46 "Get ___!" ("calm down!")
48 One more beeping thing to worry about
50 Spandex
51 Regal splendor
52 Braced, as with booze
53 Naked
54 Cat genus
55 Salt Lake player
56 *Damn Yankees* vamp
58 Maladjusted one
61 Nine-day prayer
63 Arson, for one
64 Clinton's first Defense chief
67 Secretion-related
69 Roman ag-goddess
70 Famous gym, Vic ___
72 1969 Alan Arkin film
73 He or she: abbr.
74 Semiprecious stone
76 Oscar ___ Renta
79 Tea addition
81 Yes ___
82 Shoulder enlargers
83 Lift resistance
85 City near Chicago
87 Big name in bags
88 Kirk Douglas chin feature
89 Celebrates acrobatically
90 Entrance signals
91 Caterpillar or tadpole
94 Animal adjective ending
98 He gets no respect
99 Detergent brand
100 Real-life initials of Laura Petrie
102 "I Only Have ___ You"
103 Some sleeves
104 Babe's master
106 *Showing emphasis: abbr.*
107 "Gracious!"
109 Governor of Texas (1890-95) or his daughter Ima
110 "What ___!" (reaction to a big favor)
111 Jeans pioneer Strauss
112 "Go right ___"
114 Huge ref. work
116 Vaccines
119 Not in time
121 Postage ___
123 Ukraine uh-uh
124 A Khan

ACROSS

1 Times up
7 Sound of a French financier being hit on the head?
11 Mu ___ pork
14 North Pole addressee
19 Hot pink or lime green
21 Faucet
22 Red as ___
23 The Joker on TV's *Batman*
24 Position statements
26 Make out
27 Poet's foot
28 Like the relationship of two architects in love
30 Prop for Arnie
31 ___ latté (popular hot drink, Italian-style)
33 Where the furnace is, usually
35 "___ Nagila" (traditional Jewish song)
36 Perceptive
38 Getting involved (in) superficially
39 "Sure! *No problema!*"
40 Like a new penny
41 Certain layers in shoes
42 Put into words
44 Holler mate

45 One with his ear to the ground
46 Enter stealthily
47 North extension
48 One of a flamenco pair
49 Stripping Mr. Peanut
50 Tough exams, for some
52 Rodomontade
53 Yeses
54 Trust in
55 SST
57 Testing, as mattresses, kid-style
60 Shapes of some lenses
61 Major mistakes
62 Celeb
64 Claimed to be, in court
65 Members of the house
66 Price of rice, maybe
67 *NewsHour* host
68 Windy, as a day or a senator
69 Shimon who schmoozes with Shamir
70 Lubricates
71 Flaw finders
72 Dickens's *Little ___*
73 Metry preceder
74 Some wall installers
75 Atomic chain-reaction pioneer
76 Try: abbr.

77 Showed off
78 Victuals
79 Short on watts
82 Itty-bitty
84 Sabin's breakthrough
88 Trial partner
89 Scot's negative
90 Transmission devices
91 In Rome, it means "stone," not "back talk"
92 Jerk
93 Extra costs
94 Benson partner

DOWN

1 First-grade lesson
2 The monkey puzzle, for example
3 Angle operations
4 A Khan
5 Boy Scout Law item
6 Rake with gunfire
7 75 Across helped build a big one
8 Pub pint
9 Neither trailer
10 Jolly Roger features
11 More like a Sharon Stone love scene
12 Accelerates
13 Increasing

14 Bass or Bellow
15 Sit-ups tone 'em
16 Shipshape
17 Airing
18 Classic documentary, *Victory ___*
20 Make it
25 Meal or cake opener
29 Bit of buckshot
32 Nefertiti, to Tut
33 Indecorousness
34 Betakes (oneself) away
35 Mercenary
36 Tennis star who took his apartheid fight to the United Nations
37 "See the USA" singer
38 Stretches out
39 "Freak Brothers" creator Gilbert and *Bull Durham* director Ron
41 Noted talking horse
42 Blends beforehand, as yogurt
43 Chang's twin
45 Stays the night
46 Division of Great Britain's High Court of Justice
48 Waterfalls
49 Water-depth announcers
51 *Teatro ___* (opera house in Naples)
52 Cads, or cats, sometimes
54 Wooer
55 Beetles' order
56 Near-perfect games
57 Left in a rocket
58 Primary
59 Certain Japanese-American
60 Klinger's rank: abbr.
61 Pierre who wrote *The Bridge on the River Kwai* and *Planet of the Apes*
63 Location of the sentry
65 Indigo D&C No. 6 and others
66 Salon offering
68 Woody Allen comedy featuring Howard Cosell
69 Volkswagen inventor's other car
71 Cooked cereal or Little Rascal
72 Unhook
73 Joyce Carol or Warren
74 Riley or Robertson
75 Bean preferred by Hannibal Lecter
77 The "fire" type of maniac
78 *Desire Under the ___*
80 Arrow poison
81 State of disarray
83 Ph. directory contents
85 Charlotte of *Car 54, Where Are You?*
86 Jack's weapon in *The Shining*
87 *El ___*

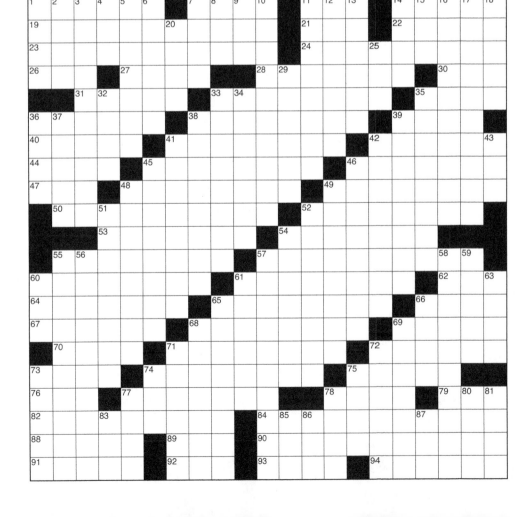

57 Great Delivery

...No one could lick Elvis, until now

ACROSS

1 Arctic birds
5 Of the ear
9 "If ___ be so bold ..."
13 Alaska adjective
18 Response to a Dear John letter? (1961)
21 Ooh trailer
22 Mediterranean tree
23 What it takes to mail things? (1956)
24 The Postmaster General? (1967)
26 Spring for (dinner)
27 Armada's milieu
29 Cigar contents, in Calais
30 Bill's *Hulk* costar
32 Lonely Street address? (1956)
39 Furniture designer William
41 Of wings
42 Regret
43 Prime seat
44 Farmer's name, in cartoons
45 Shove off
47 Postal carrier's worry? (1956)
51 Certain women's wear
53 Typewriter feature
54 Roughly
55 "Wild Bill" Donovan's org.
56 Peace, to Pushkin
57 Monopoly imperative
60 Postal guy? (1968)
62 Court ace Andre
64 Backer
66 Green situation
67 Calf catcher
71 Debt marker
72 Mail containing X's and O's? (1966)
76 Son of Adam
77 Burners named for a volcano
79 Part of a German name
80 One of Henry's six
81 Type of income or result
83 With 96 Across, a postal order? (1962)
85 Turkey Day device
87 Gob's agreement
88 Noted *numero*
91 Corduroy ridge
92 Airline to Tokyo
94 Mohammed's flight
96 See 83 Across
98 Meager poker hand
101 Four Seasons hit
103 Grandson of Adam
104 Murphy's show
105 Noted *nummer*
106 The Man of baseball
107 Possible requirement of postal inspectors? (1969)
113 Decorator's asset
114 Tomato impact
115 Puncture preceder
116 Richard Dysart TV series
120 Mail carrier's condition after a 47 Across run-in? (1957)
125 Inspiration for the 15 songs in this puzzle
129 "Swell!"
130 Monarch's address
131 Like stubborn stamps? (1960)
132 Opening
133 Four follower
134 Candy company
135 Russian poet Mandelstam

DOWN

1 Intent
2 Project Blue Book listing
3 Something that won't deter a mail carrier? (1970)
4 Prophet
5 Workplace watchdog: abbr.
6 Not dangerous
7 ___ Saud
8 Sid, Julius, and a salad
9 16 oz.
10 ___ d'
11 Pond plants
12 Start of a Flintstonism
13 Painter Hieronymus
14 VP namesakes
15 Actress Basinger
16 Hungarian sister
17 Animal refuge
19 Caustic stuff
20 Color changer
25 Popular wood
28 Skylit courts
30 White Diamonds lady
31 How long Express Mail takes? (1958)
33 Put it away
34 Gladiolus-to-be
35 Previous
36 Uproar
37 They're esteem-powered
38 What 51 Across cover
40 Fanged danger for divers
41 Slow as ___
46 Wisp of an island
47 Sellers of 51 Across
48 Abalone, to a Brit
49 This land is your land
50 Steelers coach Chuck who won four Super Bowls
52 Photo ___ (PR ploys)
56 Spice with a wallop?
58 Taste lover
59 Early astronaut
60 Extremely
61 Portland OR to Portland ME
63 Shiner of a sort
65 Slangy affirmative
68 Shipping by land or air? (1972)
69 Mail carrier's words to a 47 Across? (1968)
70 "___ Who Tread the Narrow Way" (Kipling)
73 Little egg
74 Work on this
75 Derisive responses
78 Like a quilt
82 Work unit
84 Smidge
86 Deli-cutter option
88 Salt Lake players
89 Lower-class, in Britain
90 Mexican honey-lovers
92 Pleasures
93 Feminine side, to Jung
95 37 Down counterparts
97 Feat of thought
99 Next-to-last syllables
100 Assistance
102 Travel dir.
104 It's coming
108 "___ an arrow ..."
109 USN rank
110 Kael's ___ *It at the Movies*
111 Jack of *The Great Dictator*
112 Cold desserts
117 Pops the question
118 British ensemble that Previn once led: abbr.
119 ___ extra cost
120 It often comes between two people
121 Civil War figure
122 Testing place
123 VW intro?
124 The write thing
126 Sight, on the Seine
127 Pronoun, on the Seine
128 Doggie

ACROSS

1 Early wake-up call
7 *Frankenstein, ___ Modern Prometheus*
12 Rabbit run
15 Onset of cold
19 Valley girl's reaction to her first beer?
21 Mock, in a way
22 It makes a freeway into a feeway
23 The ___ (bending the elbow?)
25 TV Johnny, the rebel
26 "Star Wars," really: abbr.
27 Global turning point
28 Tyson's home, for a while
29 Pig Latin cancellation
30 Con vote
32 Rattles
36 Lethargy
39 Beer-lover's dinner?
45 *North by Northwest* star's first name
46 Guam et al.
48 Feathered "friend"?
50 Beery attorney?
52 Swiss river
55 Forty-___
56 Memo opener
57 On the tip of
58 "___ the bag"
60 See 45 Across
61 Start of a Shakespeare comedy
63 What Rip Taylor says even when he's on the wagon?
66 With 71 Across, a beer drinker's bio?
71 See 66 Across
74 Ataturk's first
79 Tranquillity Base place
80 Last letter
81 Sandy getaway
85 Go over again
86 Llama land
88 Top number?
89 Bit of grade-B entertainment for beer drinkers?
92 Brosnan's sleuth
94 Jonathan Kozol classic, *Death at an ___*
95 Allen or Robbins
96 Smarter about beer?
100 Subaru model
102 Memory-testing game show hosted by Bill Cullen, 1966-69
103 Last one to know
104 Outfit
108 East of Eden brother
109 Street-name word
112 Startling syllable
115 Fontanne's guy
116 One-beer bars?
122 Slaw, for one
123 Pay this: abbr.
124 Getting romantic in a bar?
125 Split this
126 Country contest
127 Indian or Korean
128 Respect

DOWN

1 Three after E
2 Angers
3 Invalid
4 Ocean phenom
5 Enzyme tail
6 Jim of ABC Sports
7 Everything: prefix
8 Evidence of dreaming
9 ___ degree
10 Slangy Nazi
11 Time for *vacances*
12 Must
13 First game
14 For each
15 A river, or Nike's mother
16 Part of speech
17 Mahler's mate (who later married Walter Gropius)
18 Recreation
20 Spell
24 Doing
29 "What ___ without the beasts?" (Chief Seattle)
31 Join this
32 Zoic preceder
33 Closely trimmed, as meat
34 Anti-smoking org.
35 Queue after Q
36 Old photo tint
37 Pizzeria appliances
38 Fend off a fencer
39 Jog
40 Hawaii city
41 Scrape with a file
42 Susan's Kane
43 Desilu partner
44 Suspicious
47 Doctors' org.
49 Like some beers
51 1906 car
52 Bulletin board abbr.
53 In ___ (very soon)
54 Vex
58 "The wolf ___ the door"
59 Milit. person
62 Ashes holder
63 Palindromic Swedish group
64 Malaprop or Robinson
65 '60s Atty. General
67 Impediment to humility
68 Calibration: abbr.
69 Saber alternative
70 Attractive quality?: abbr.
71 TV sidekick in buckskin
72 Reagan's third Interior secretary
73 "___ a vacation!"
75 Pull a boner
76 Grocery section
77 Let in or on
78 Like clay
79 Rustic parents
81 Drug abuse, discrimination, etc.
82 Leonard ___ (Roy Rogers)
83 Regan's dad
84 Work unit
87 Stay down, as a yo-yo
89 Murray and West
90 Eye part
91 ___ *vu*
93 Station ending
94 Fleecy one
97 Grew into
98 Peter Lorre in *Casablanca*
99 Unexciting
101 Snare hit, usually
103 Level
104 Mrs. Charles Laughton
105 Walk out
106 Free, in a way
107 News tidbit
109 Earth goddess
110 Opposite of "fer"
111 Amtrak stop: abbr.
113 "Coffee, tea, ___?"
114 Free, in a way
116 Truck part
117 ___ Na Na
118 Derek doubles
119 Mr. Wallach
120 Letters on a video
121 Scud missile, for one: abbr.

Leveling the Playing Field   ...Hope everything goes smoothly

ACROSS

1 Scarred skipper
5 Buying binge, e.g.
10 Little we know?
14 Quits abruptly
19 River of shadoofs
20 Surface-___ missile
21 Say that again
22 Say good night to her
23 Leveled 1984 sci-fi film?
25 Anna's adopted land
26 S.F. player
27 Chi players
28 Faces in the ring
29 Leveled engineering wonder?
31 Upriver spawner
32 Peer group?
33 Algonquin Hotel regulars, once
34 Leveled Cooper character?
37 Took off
38 Kachina doll maker
39 A gender: abbr.
42 Lake Indians
43 1976 pop hit, "___ Gone"
44 Leveled celebration?
46 Teen tormentor
47 Dinner downer
49 Prolix
50 Dissipated one
51 Leveled driver?
53 Casual greeting
54 *My Darling Clementine* star
55 Simple fellow
56 Fountain order
57 Homer or Moses
59 TV alien
62 Leveled presiding officer?
65 Steam sound
66 Adenauer's nickname
68 Tender promises?
69 Question relentlessly
71 Flabbergasted
72 ___ A to Z
73 Leveled parts of a meal?
77 She sailed in 1492
78 Did a cobbler's job
80 Dannay and Lee's sleuth
81 *Charles in Charge* star
82 Fails, in a leveled way?
84 Contemptible ones
85 Golden Fleece co-conspirator
86 Type units
87 Broke ground, in a way
88 It holds water
89 Leveled capital of Malaysia?
91 Utah park
92 Gerald or Patrick preceder
93 Word on a john door
94 In level terms, what "the problems of three little people" don't do "in this crazy woild"?

98 Ball marrier
99 Possesses
102 Arnold's mate
103 Aware of
104 Leveled utterer of 94 Across (in a 1942 classic)?
106 Syndicated seer
107 With -tine, a drink
108 *Barry Lyndon* lead
109 "Goodness!"
110 Rented again
111 Michelle Pfeiffer in *Batman Returns*, Selina ___
112 "No man is an island" author
113 Cameo stone

DOWN

1 Raid targets
2 Cracker brand
3 *A Clockwork Orange*'s main character
4 Trifecta, for one
5 Silkwood portrayer
6 Grapefruit
7 Her *Nick of Time* album won four Grammys
8 Beethoven's one
9 Would-be 27th Amdt.
10 Vacation location
11 In an unkind way
12 African nation
13 Certain assignments
14 Man's shoe
15 Te Kanawa recordings
16 Mardi Gras follower
17 Vulnerable joint, in sports
18 Herzegovina hardliner
24 Tube honors
29 .38s and .45s
30 On the brisk side
31 Handles the wheel
32 Taunt
34 Almost here
35 Paris landmark
36 Get ideas, to Muggsy?
37 "Stop pouring now"
38 ___-Hoop
39 Phony companies, often
40 Piano pieces
41 "I can't believe ___!"
43 Pool member
44 Doctor's order
45 *East of Eden* twin
47 Actor M. ___ Walsh
48 Lady of Spain, I do this to you
49 They're high and low
52 Popcorn-carrier's path
53 Boring
54 Catch and throw
56 Didn't run
57 Blender setting
58 Born in Baghdad or Bangkok
59 Rodgers and Hart tune, "Ten Cents ___"
60 French award, the ___ of Honor
61 Monet's money
63 Canner?
64 Charm-challenged fairy-tale beings
67 On ___ with
70 Fashion I.D.s
72 Took off
73 Knot in cloth (or a noted singer-actor's first name)
74 Zip, to Zapata
75 God, to Godard
76 Bust out laughing
78 *Airplane!*, e.g.
79 Type of test
80 Type of test
83 Company that makes the Etch-A-Sketch
84 Lloyd Webber hit
85 Passover food
88 Ground-corn flour
89 African coffee
90 Helpless
91 African country
92 ___ *Attraction*
93 Like Mr. Spock's blood
94 Love god
95 Domesticate
96 Type of test
97 A Deadly Sin
98 Florence's river
99 Bakker's Jessica
100 Navy foe?
101 Charon's river
104 Mason's prop
105 Sticky stuff

ACROSS

1 Cause of cling
7 Amenhotep was one
14 Ristorante rundown
20 Yacht spot
21 Otalgia
22 Emulate Vlad
23 Emetic plant
24 Jefferson's second VP
25 Actor Anthony
26 Holiday in Hué
27 Invite
29 5-centime piece
31 Abner's radio chum
32 "Whadja say?"
33 Do one's thing as a responsible citizen (continues at 39 Down, backwards to 105, and up to 33 to form a square around the "X")
40 *To a Skylark*, e.g.
41 Bowler's save
43 Corporate head
44 No turns ___
46 And the rest, briefly
48 Closet skeletons
49 Stop for the Sunset Ltd.
50 Word coined by Frank Lloyd Wright
54 Great effort
55 Controversial injection
59 Lager cousin
60 Small glass vessel
62 Some chart checkers, familiarly
63 Young Cleaver, to Wally
64 Introduction to corn?
65 Sloppiness safeguard
66 Fix firmly
68 See 84 Across
69 Some Sun. successes
70 Hemic trio
71 On a slant
72 Jewelry-case liner, often
73 First of the double digits
74 Certain microchip
75 Top
77 Maigret's river
78 Woodpile tool
79 Recession
80 Fermentation vessels
81 Truth, in Tiananmen Square
83 Serb or Croat
84 With 68 Across, a Bogart-Robinson film
85 Mortarboard features
87 Break in shooting
89 They play to the balcony
91 "___ the pits"
92 He never drinks ... wine
94 A letter from Lesbos
95 Nickname of basketballer Maurice Stokes
98 Lacking decorum
100 Strip of membership
104 Suffix for collectibles
105 See 33 Down
108 Duarte of Argentina
109 High school debate org.
110 Janitor's prop
111 Kamchatka bird
112 Type of point or theory
113 Last king of England
116 Bellerophon's mount
122 Victoria's consort
125 Breadwinner
126 Part of EKG
127 Dr. Seuss turtle
128 Exquisite
129 Eats in front of the TV
130 Animal Shelter truckload

DOWN

1 Commonfolk?
2 Get ready for UPS
3 Soulful Franklin
4 Nervous reaction
5 Concert finale?
6 Chocolate source
7 Birds, at times
8 Henry V's nickname
9 Tanker guy
10 Campaigned (for)
11 Use the Method
12 Cry of discovery
13 Muppet family?
14 Arouse
15 ___ Darya (Asian river)
16 Home-gym alternative
17 "Old Rough and Ready"
18 Make reference
19 Appeared
28 "The Racer's Edge"
30 He had 511 career homers
33 Do one's thing as Chief Executive (continues at 105 Across, etc.)
34 Second in command
35 First name in bologna
36 Flagging
37 Idyllic places
38 Racetrack docs
39 See 33 Across
42 House mbr.
45 Ford's 34 Down: inits.
47 Big House members
49 Whoopi Goldberg, to Caryn Johnson
50 Euro-nightspot
51 Woodcutter in *The Arabian Nights*
52 Orders a second strike on
53 Forms of relief?
55 Like a lackey
56 Face on the cutting-room floor
57 Librarian, at times
58 Walt, Roy, et al.
61 "___ pray"
63 Cotton collections
67 Barney Fife, for one: abbr.
68 Guitarist Paul
76 A real turn-on?
81 Draw around
82 Prefix meaning "eye"
86 Actor Alastair
87 Type of agency or trailer: abbr.
88 Abbr. on a mountain sign
90 A tribute to the way things are run?
92 Kicked off the ticket
93 "To everything there is ___"
95 Hit hard
96 "... that England should crouch down ___ and yield" (Shak.)
97 Anagram of AL GORE
98 Old Pontiac model
99 Mr. Symington
101 Spanish money unit
102 Vocalist Don or Phil
103 Relatives of cappuccinos
106 Abrasive substance
107 Approves
114 Essential cell component
115 Tourmaline or turquoise
117 Clark and Marilyn's *Misfits* co-star
118 H. Norman was one
119 Sky king?
120 They usually run E and W
121 Tell tale site?
123 Permit
124 Cold remark?

HURRICANE PUZZLES

These puzzles, which first appeared in American crossword magazines around 1980, will "have you coming and going," but hopefully in a good way. In the puzzle world they are known simply as "spirals," but when I was asked to make them for a newspaper in Florida I decided to give them a more Florida-related name — hurricane puzzles, since the answers spiral much like hurricane winds do.

Here's how to play:

The Inward answers start at square 1 and spiral toward the center, one letter per square. The Outward answers start at square 100 and spiral outward. The clue numbers denote the starting square and ending square of each answer. Words going one way will help you get words going the other way. Solutions are at the back of the book.

Tell us what you think at www.sundaycrosswords.com — "contact Merl."

THE HURRICANE

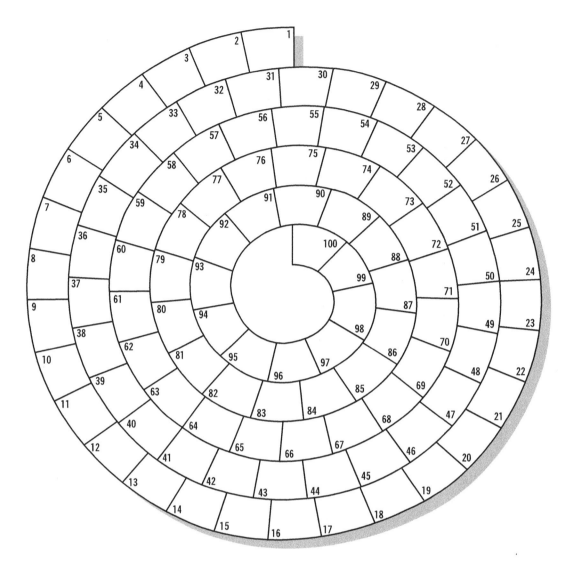

INWARD

1-5   Stick-on design
6-12   Son of Zeus who slew
       Medusa
13-17 Ten Commandments site,
       Mount ___
18-24 Some Spanish speakers
25-31 Relaxing rubdown
32-35 Pull along the ground
36-40 Ex-Yankee Jeter
41-48 King Lear's youngest
       daughter
49-55 Rudolph's bright feature
       (2 words)
56-63 Ernest of the movies
64-71 Explorer for whom
       America is named

72-76 Hirsute
77-82 Mrs. Kowalski in a
       Williams play
83-86 Greek letter
87-94 Mosque spires
95-100 More courageous

OUTWARD

100-91 Chain with the motto
       "Seafood Differently"
       (2 words)
90-84 Bring to life, as cartoons
83-78 "The Nutcracker," e.g.
77-73 Middle East country
72-66 Involuntary actions often
       caused by carbonated
       beverages or hot peppers

65-59 6:30 broadcast, the ___
       news
58-52 Paul who sang "Ol' Man
       River" in "Show Boat"
51-44 Ran off the tracks
43-38 Moving chair for
       grandma
37-28 French painter whose
       first name is almost an
       anagram of his last
       name (2 words)
27-22 Bible figure who had a
       bad hair day
21-15 Like Columbus or
       Fellini
14-9   Copies of the paper
8-1   Stood in for

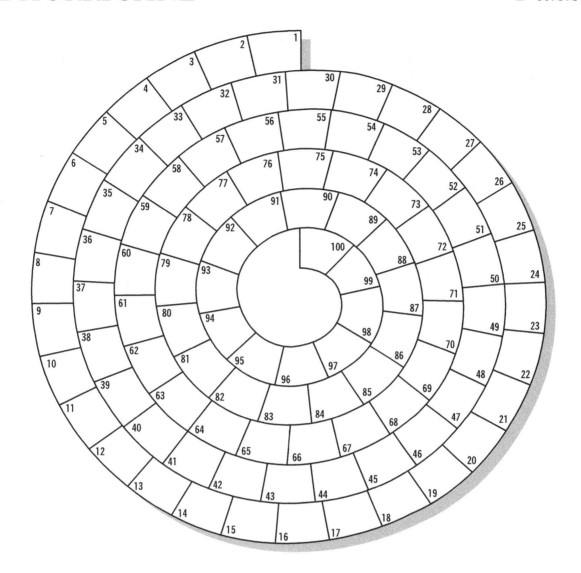

INWARD

1-5	Encounters
6-11	Search ___ (online aid)
12-16	Sired, in the Bible
17-24	Amorous missive (2 words)
25-30	House of cards?
31-37	Work perk for young parents (2 words)
38-41	Money drawer
42-47	Mount Carmel's country
48-55	Cover with clear plastic
56-61	Attacked by vampires, say
62-69	Co-star of "The Godfather" (2 words)
70-76	Part of "IRS"
77-81	Fruity spread
82-89	Didn't go
90-100	Street urchins

OUTWARD

100-96	Check the smell of
95-93	Actress Thurman
92-85	Fragrant white flower
84-80	Sophie's portrayer
79-73	Marine Corps training base in North Carolina, Camp ___
72-65	Lake in Hollywood?
64-59	Venus, for one
58-52	Like Shih Tzus and the Dalai Lama
51-43	"You've got my attention; tell me more!" (3 words)
42-33	Inability to read
32-27	Gorgeous Greek of yore
26-20	Ingredient in nail polish remover
19-13	Amount of power in an electric current
12-7	Kindly
6-1	High regard

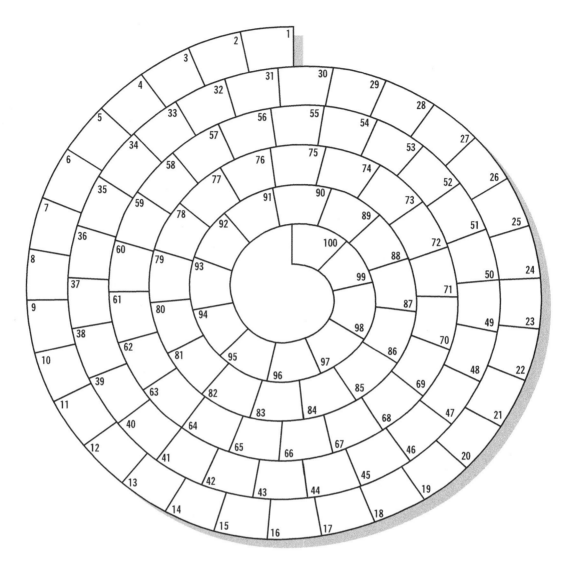

INWARD

1-10	Violin maker (1644-1737)
11-18	Ex-New York City mayor who appeared in a *Seinfeld* episode
19-23	Sans-___ type
24-30	Author Georges who created Inspector Maigret
31-36	College graduates
37-45	Tears to pieces (2 words)
46-51	Black, gooey spot where fossils are sometimes found (2 words)
52-56	Persian Gulf emirate
57-62	Fearsome African fly
63-66	Artist featured in a St. Petersburg museum
67-72	Fasten
73-77	Longtime Yankees manager Joe
78-83	Actress Bondi who played James Stewart's mother in *It's A Wonderful Life*
84-88	High-calorie cake
89-93	Gabriel of *The Usual Suspects*
96-100	Major Houlihan's nickname on *M*A*S*H* (2 words)

OUTWARD

100-96	"Don't cry over ___ milk"
95-90	Author of *The Gift of the Magi* and other ironic-twist stories (2 words)
89-81	Engagement to be married
80-72	Peter who organized the 1984 Summer Olympics in Los Angeles and became baseball commissioner that same year
71-65	Marsh plant with a feline name
64-59	The other name of "O Come All Ye Faithful," "___ Fideles"
58-53	Layers, as of rock
52-49	Popular cotton-swab brand
48-42	Filthy, run-down building, so-called from its rodent population
41-35	Headache reliever
34-30	Animated 1998 Disney film based on a Chinese folktale
29-27	"The loneliest number"
26-20	Fail to discharge, as a gun
19-15	Egypt's ___ Peninsula
14-10	Mario's Nintendo brother, or playwright Pirandello
9-6	Sitar legend Shankar
5-1	Popular pub game

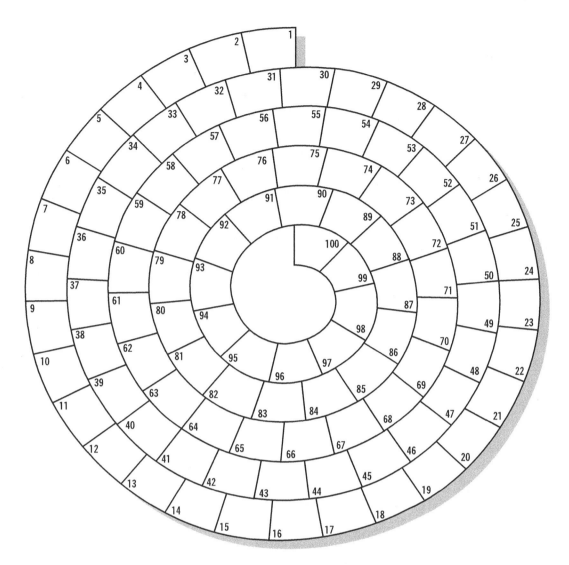

INWARD

1-8   Pertaining to meaning

9-14   The Big Ten's Fighting ___

15-23   Piece of land that juts out into the water, such as Florida

24-30   Unintended silence during a radio broadcast (2 words)

31-37   With ice cream (3 words)

38-47   Living matter in cells

48-52   Cake tier

53-56   Actress Rowlands

57-62   Brand name of a popular hay fever and allergy drug

63-72   Combines into a whole

73-79   Sicilian seaport that Patton famously "reached first"

80-86   Greet like a suspicious dog (2 words)

87-90   ___ facto

91-95   Wreak ___ (cause destruction)

96-100   Actor Sebastian

OUTWARD

100-94   Snuff stuff

93-84   Military health care facility (3 words, with abbr.)

83-78   Abductor's demand

77-71   Slip back, as into an illness

70-65   It may have a bull's-eye

64-58   Encouraging comment to someone who just missed the mark (2 words)

57-50   Author of "Riders of the Purple Sage" (2 words)

49-46   "___ for the poor ..."

45-42   Rival of Iams and Ken-L Ration

41-35   Submarine weapon

34-28   What quinine treats

27-20   Father of Icarus who fashioned his son's wax wings

19-13   One of ten, in bowling

12-6   Not legal

5-1   Tom, Dick, and Harry, e.g.

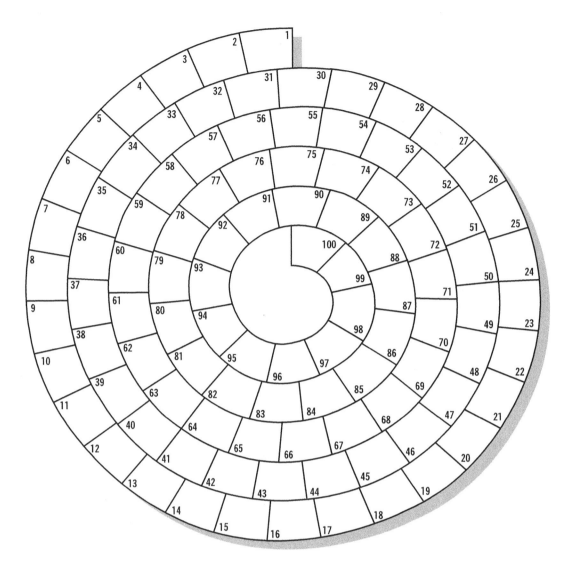

INWARD

1-8   Groups of attendants who follow and look after VIPs

9-13   Rescuer

14-21   Words that look similar from language to language

22-28   Winnerless way that some chess games end (3 words)

29-36   Tarts, tiramisu, etc.

37-44   Orchestra leaders

45-49   Under way

50-54   Godzilla's stomping ground

55-58   Sassy kid

59-64   Nonprofessional people

65-73   Former comedy partner of Mike Nichols (2 words)

74-76   In the style of (2 words)

77-82   Music key whose signature has five sharps (2 words)

83-86   Singer Fitzgerald

87-94   Publisher's stock of not-new but still-available books

95-100   Reagan's predecessor

OUTWARD

100-94   Take back, as a statement

93-90   Parachute fabric

89-81   Spanish gentleman or horseman

80-72   Cajun dish of rice, shellfish, and chicken

71-66   Lowly, as some tasks

65-61   Adversary

60-53   Often young assistant at a Mass (2 words)

52-48   Actor Yaphet who played Agent Mosely in "Midnight Run"

47-41   To some degree (3 words)

40-31   Woman who sews

30-25   He gave up the throne for Wallis

24-20   Licorice-flavored seed

19-15   "It takes two to ___"

14-7   Deep fissure, as in a glacier

6-1   One who brings people together

ANSWERS

1 Stakeout!

```
SPAS  RAVI  SPAM   SADAT
ALIT  AMID  TAXI   APLANE
GODISMYCOPILOT     SALVOS
SPACES    ARON  FAT  IRT
    KEEL  SLUM  JAB  DDAY
TOFU  SYNCOPATEDCLOCK
HARPO RIOS  RED   ADO
AHA  SEIKO  JOEPISCOPO
TUN  CACOPHONY  ELK  PIG
  CZAR  LEASE  STY  MENU
CRIER  TARN  SITS  CORKY
HOSE  DOI  GEESE  CHEF
ETC  MOB  MARCOPOLO  ISH
  COMICOPERA  TOTUP  EAU
  POD  GOT  POUT  SPLIT
  DIVINGSEACOPTER  ODDS
SIZE  OAT  BAKE  ROAR
AVA  MTN  SAME  NASSAU
FERGIE  UNDERCOVERCOPS
ERRAND  FOAL  AXEL  HUED
STOLE  OWNS  BOXY  ELSA
```

2 Country Couples

```
BID  TIMES  KAL  ADJUST
ARAT  OFART  IDO  BEAGLE
SAMOACHILE  LOS  BYMAIL
KENYASENEGAL  THE  ANTE
  LAI  OBJ  WESAID
LANA  NATO  COCOA  SCARF
EDENS  LOUT  YARD  PALER
CHADANDORRA  SLA  SKATE
HOT  FOAL  AND  DCS  OOID
COLAS  OTITIS  HEARSE
  IRANWALESGREECE
MOBILE  BERATE  SCANT
DEMY  EWE  REV  HATE  ARK
ISAAC  SLY  MONACOSUDAN
DONHO  ROAM  WISE  SNIDE
ANNUM  ONMAN  PHDS  CREW
  ONALOG  ROB  HAL
BORG  IMA  GHANABOLIVIA
ASWARM  TWO  SYRIASPAIN
SHARON  EAT  ISALL  SNIT
SAYYES  DRS  CELLS  SIS
```

3 I Fill Your Pain

```
THEEGG  ELI  SULU  OMEN
ROLLIE  DAIS  TRILOBITE
ORALROBERTS  ONESPLATE
TAN  DRILLTEAMS  TEASED
HIDALGO  OLIVA  HENS
  LEE  ABE  ALLER  TITO
BAJA  PAVERS  ORSO  RUG
UTA  AUTO  PRODS  IRATE
SONINLAW  BRONZEPLAQUE
MEDAL  APOISE  LOCI
  THEMILLONTHEFLOSS
  ARAM  OTTERS  ILIKE
COTTONMATHER  ASSONANT
HOREB  UNSER  LAHR  TOW
AZO  EIRE  SPEEDO  PESO
SYNC  SETHS  ANN  NSA
  ITAS  UINTA  SECRETE
SNAPIT  UNDERBRUSH  XIS
ESCHEWING  WILLIAMHURT
GUMERASER  ACES  COULEE
OBER  ROSY  TED  TSETSE
```

4 Dinner and a Movie

```
INGE  MAE  ELAINE  DOW
MEATBALLS  AVENGES  END
THETOASTOFNEWYORK  MAS
ORLESS  ONION  DIGIT
OUS  ORAN  SAAB  METER
  ONEPOTATOTWOPOTATO
VOLUME  ALI  AERO  SHY
VICERING  STOLENKISSES
CDC  SNARL  HRE  ELMER
REUBENREUBEN  ATSEA
ORR  MAMA  OAHU  ZOA
ODIST  BUTTERFIELD8
MACON  SYN  MANIN  IDO
PORKCHOPHILL  DIVULGES
URB  OKIE  IES  NESTOR
  FRIEDGREENTOMATOES
FITTO  ASTA  NONO  FOO
CROUP  IDIOT  ALARUM
BOA  BREADANDCHOCOLATE
ING  TOSTADA  HEARTBURN
ZEE  SPEEDS  RKO  ADES
```

5 Anagram Nicknames

```
  HUG  LOOK  GRR  MOLARS
AMAHL  ASHE  LOO  ARABIC
CARFINSCOPPOLA  SILICA
ADD  BETA  TUBERS  KEATON
REID  ERRS  REX  CELL
RINALDO  PASS  PAD  ASIA
ORGIESLEONE  SAMMS  END
TASSE  EDIT  SIR  AINTWE
  ERA  SLIMESTANDISH
FORSALE  ALAIN  LAID
UNO  TATERWILLIAMS  ITE
REDD  TIEIN  PEEBLES
  MEANMULELEWIS  AMY
ZINNIA  EFT  WRAP  ASTRI
ALT  TREES  AIRGERSHWIN
PESO  KAN  BRIE  EASIEST
  NEER  CUE  GILD  PEKE
NOLARDPALMER  BAIO  ZEN
INAJAM  HELLYESWINTERS
RENATA  MAE  AREA  MORSE
OREGON  ENG  NYNY  EMS
```

6 Presidential Pizza Party

```
DAM  ALAS  OGPU  BATFOR
EMU  ASABC  DEAN  ORIOLE
FILLMOREORDERS  PEARLS
ATTAINS  POLKCHOPS  DIO
TYING  RUBY  HALE  SKED
  SOCIAL  VERNON
JACKSONBALANCES  AROSE
ABUY  USE  OCEAN  WRECKS
MOB  CLU  ORBS  THY  KIP
BUSHCOMESTOSHOVE  ISMY
  ALUMNA  INTROS
EDGY  REAGANINTHEDOUGH
VAR  FIR  EXIT  EWE  RIO
ARAMIS  ILLBE  IMA  PILL
SENOR  HAYESMAKESWASTE
  TOMTOM  ROSIER
TEST  HAWS  GWEN  STPAT
ILL  NIXONCUTS  SATIATE
AVATAR  MADISONCABINET
REMAPS  AKID  LEARY  TAR
ASSIST  NEMO  DATE  YMA
```

7 — Sorry, Wrong Letter Again!

```
CREED  CORAL  OSLO   TREE
HENRI  ANISE  FLANAHEAD
APAIN  LEOTARDODAVINCI
POCKETVITO OATS  INTHE
SST  DIES  SPY   ASK
  SOBS  BPOE   DAN  STOP
ACTONE VIOL  SOLTI  HBO
DAHL THEBRONTOSISTERS
ALE  EXIT  AERO  NOWAY
MYST ARE  ASIA   UTAH
EXPO PARKBELLIES  DINO
  ATME  ELAH  NYE  SNOW
OHWHY DUNE  EASE   INN
MOOERSANDSHAKERS ONCE
ALL AUDIO  EDIT  MERGER
REFS BAT  ASSN   RUNG
  HAJ  RLS   CARD   ADD
CODEX GUAM  COLDFINGER
ITALIANSCALLION  NOLIE
ROWVSWADE PASSE  GRETA
CONE ERAS  SNEER  SATYR
```

8 — It's Only Money

```
PCT  SLID  FILIAL  TPS
OHO  PESOWECANGO  HOHOS
WAMPUMONTHEHEAD  ARENA
 PHENOM ORATE  KICKED
AMON NET  GIDEON  HEM
BARNEYRUBLE  POI   LOS
ANNEX BEE  ELIOT  SARA
  TAM  REUNES  SIDNEY
 DROPYOURPENCE  LIDDY
BILLOWS TRI  COL  HIE
CANS DOUBLOONMAN  RIMS
AHA FAR  RAP  AREMADE
STRAY KRONAMUSTACHE
ASITIS ONERUN  ELK
BISE EPICS NUT  ABHOR
AMS  GAL  TIMOTHYLIRA
PEN ANSARA  POE  ILIE
ISRAEL LENDL  BATTLE
LOVIN PFENNIGSARIZONA
KNEAD RUPEEKEELER CTR
 DDS ONHERE  WIRE  KEY
```

9 — Bow Wow Wow

```
 CONES GEO  GBS   SCARS
TOTORECALL ROE  ACACIA
ASTABEHOMESOON  CALLON
UTAH DEL  SANDYCLAUSE
TAW APT  DAWNS  ARAM
 RADIO MAC  GNU   AGO
 ORDOIHAVETOGETRUFF
EYRE ALLNIGHT  AIMTO
LOU WET ALAR  RAG  BEG
FUTBOL FALADIRECTIONS
 URACIL   FESTER
GRANDTHEFTOTTO  OAKIER
OAF SEE RARE  ARM  ANA
TOAST RERENTED  ANDY
OUCHOUCHDAMNEDSPOT
 LEE PRO   ITS  EDITH
 MISO CEASE ARE   HIM
NANASECONDS  INF  CEDE
AMULET NOSHIRTNOSHOES
RIDERS UTE  NOCERBERUS
REESE  SEL  NTH  MARYS
```

10 — Little Stinker

```
 LEMONTEA     ORIOLE
AMATEURS PTSD  LANVIN
PROVOUTAH RAKE ARDENT
RATEOF PRIMITIVEURGE
OMEN SCION  LOT  RCS
 PRACTICALUSE   THIN
SON HALLS EVER TBOONE
TWOPAGE ATIT DEAREST
PETERUSTINOV DARN SOS
 DUE  ATTN  DAUNTS
 PROMETHEUSUNBOUND
 STATUE NEST   ART
WIT EDAM PICKERUPPERS
ADHERES BEVY  ULYSSES
SEEYOU PARE SARAN SEW
HATE POLYURETHANE
 ASP SAS SNAIL   PAID
PUBLICUTILITY  FROMME
ARLENE EDIT POPEURBAN
USEFOR DENY UNRENTED
LASTTO     TOYSTORE
```

11 — Brainstorm!

```
AMA WOOL  ABUT  QUI REB
GIN ANNE  SAKI  USO ORE
AGO STET  STEDAMUSCLE
TODEPOTS ICI ETC  EKES
HEEP PONTCHART   JAY
ASSAM NOOK NEO  RENTAL
 CAP TRAP  AXIOM   EGO
LEFTJAB ESTES RBI  RUG
OXO ASAD  ADOBE  MONEY
BARR SHOJI SNL   KAY
EMMA GOGER ETUDE  EWES
 ZOO MAE  LORDE   SAME
AUGER CANNY  BEND  NIX
SPO RAH NEILS  REENTRY
TOO ELATE  PANT   REO
ONFIRE WCS MOOD  PROMO
 TRY LANEWMAN   ARTY
TORO NON MOB  CLAUDES
HAUNTINGREF ALIS   LIT
AFT IKE CLUE  TALE SEE
ISH PER TEND  SSSS ERR
```

12 — Hold the Tomatoes

```
 VAT VEY  ALICE   ARAB
OVINE FLO MORON  GENES
FIVER WALDOSALT  OLIVE
FRIARS IKES  DOC  AMEN
AGAR TENSE COLMUSTARD
 INTHESEA WARY  BEETLE
INPOINT CRIME WAX  EYE
MII ROHE  ALASKA
FACET EVENLY ALUM  JOE
MKT RECTI HYDRA   OLD
LALAKER HOAGY ONASSIS
AYE AGOGO MOPUP   LEV
DOS LOLA  SHROVE TYPED
 LLAMAS APAR   HRE
MPS ACE LIMES  PLOWBOY
ARCANA BALM  EJECTION
JOHNCHEESE OVERA  ELIS
OMEN NAG  ALIT  NANOOK
ROMEO TOBYBELCH  REGNA
STEAD ENIAC LAO  ERNST
 ERLE NECKS ERG   ASA
```

13 — The Marquee de Sod

```
GOB  REM  AHA  MAJ  RADAR
ALA  EVA  VAR  ISA  OGIVE
SIR  HERBERTLOAM  ORRIN
POTTINGANDSOUL  ATITLE
OTT  RUBYS  ATUB  BAS
LAWNCHANEY  PROFUMO
ELI  HOM  CHOKE  ZIGGY
EAST  OAS  OAR  HAZZARD
RICHEARTHIII  HONI  RIS
RAF  TARN  AILS  ADD
TURFGUYSDONTDANCE
HAM  EONS  REAM  ROE
AOK  ACRE  WORMALADOUCE
THEANTS  GAP  ENE  FROM
TOTED  HAIRS  MIA  AIM
HISSING  GRASSKELLY
PSI  HAND  HAREM  DIE
UPSHOT  SOILENTRUNNING
RAJIV  SAVEMEASEED  GOO
ERODE  ANA  ACT  ATE  ONO
REBEL  MDL  SEA  DOR  RON
```

14 — Words by Design

```
IMPAIR  BANGZOOM  NITAS
MARINE  AMARILLO  ENACT
ICEMAN  DEMANDER  APNEA
TALENTS  RIDGE  TARRING
ARARE  TRIBES  PALMISTS
TOTS  LEONID  DARLIN
ENE  PAGODA  TELLASTORY
DISCOUNTS  GALLERS  VEE
AIDES  WASLOST  MESA
SPENSER  CASTORS  DARER
HALTED  BOLTERS  CARMAN
ARIES  MILLARD  CARTELS
MOOR  RAGLANS  SONNY
ALT  BERWICK  HENDERSON
NESSELRODE  RANCID  APE
CLAIRE  TOSSED  DREW
SPLATTED  DABBER  SOARS
CLOTHES  AERIE  TWINBED
RANTO  ORDAINED  IDEATE
ENGEL  FEELFINE  GLINTS
WEARE  FASTFAST  SENDAK
```

15 — Taxing Your Abilities

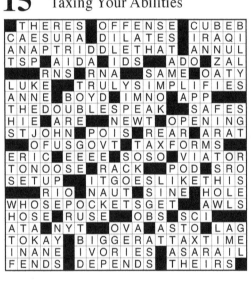

```
THERES  OFFENSE  CUBEB
CAESURA  DILATES  IRAQI
ANAPTRIDDLETHAT  ANNUL
TSP  AIDA  IDS  ADO  ZAL
RNS  RNA  SAME  OATY
LUKE  TRULYSIMPLIFIES
ANNE  BOYD  IMNO  APP
THEDOUBLESPEAK  SAFES
HIE  ARE  NEWT  OPENING
STJOHN  POIS  REAR  ARAT
OFUSGOVT  TAXFORMS
ERIC  EEEE  SOSO  VIATOR
TONOOSE  RACK  POD  SRO
SETUP  ITGOESLIKETHIS
RIO  NAUT  SINE  HOLE
WHOSEPOCKETSGET  AWLS
HOSE  RUSE  OBS  SCI
ATA  NYT  OVA  ASTO  LAG
TOKAY  BIGGERATTAXTIME
INANE  IVORIES  ASARAIL
FENDS  DEPENDS  THEIRS
```

16 — Going Up!

```
SHARERS  ALABAMA  CHAR
STARTREK  SOLARIS  HARE
PASSERBYSCOMMENT  INCA
APT  SIRLOINS  ONIT  DAS
SLED  SEAL  OVO  WALDO
MENOT  ABOUTANEWHOMEIN
NOCK  KITER  OHARAS
TIEUP  IWANNA  SUIT
SANFRANCISCO  TASTIEST
HITON  ARRET  BORES  TWA
OPER  SPIES  MUTTS  CHIC
JAN  CAPES  RIGOR  SHARK
INDULGED  WELLWELLONLY
NOIR  MALDEN  YALES
BRUISE  BASIE  GENE
YESTERDAYITWASA  TRAWL
ASHES  EBS  HAVA  ARIA
NOE  TOME  FORASONG  TNT
OURS  LOTNOWITSTOOMUCH
SNIP  ENTICED  ETAGERES
EDNA  ADELINE  DESOTOS
```

17 — My Sediments Exactly

```
PAT  SHAW  SANTE  RIVAL
ARLO  OATH  ALOHA  ABATE
SIPPINGMAGNATES  BELEM
IMALL  GERMY  MYCARD
FACESNIFFCOMPETITION
LAS  USO  OUTON  ASOF
SAT  RELACE  DEE  TRA
SOD  UBU  CORKROOMDRAMA
THINKABOUTSECS  AGE
RAGU  ROAST  DOCS  EVILS
ARID  SAX  AKA  EDIT
PANIC  TATA  ORRIN  LAVE
SOV  CARAFESMANSHIP
BOTTLEFATIGUE  SNY  ODS
ABO  ALL  TOASTS  GER
RIMS  CORAS  TUE  ERA
THEFRUITOFONESLABELS
UNIONS  ACURE  PULLA
ALLAN  DECANTBESERIOUS
CACTI  ETHIC  IOUS  LADS
EPEES  ROOMY  ASPS  DDE
```

18 — Yesterday I Looked Out a Cafe Window and Saw ...

```
THELAW  WHEAT  OTIS  LAD
NODICE  HARPO  CINA  ACE
THEFULLERBRUSHMAN  STY
ONE  SIN  RARE  DMSO
THEWOMANNEXTDOOR
ETHER  EMOTES  HUN
LOONIER  NOMY  TRINIDAD
BIRDONAWIRE  MANNEQUIN
OLDE  AMA  CLOAK  UCLA
WEEDS  BROADAX  SUE
SRS  ABOYANDHISDOG  ANG
ELL  TEENIER  HOTEL
ATTN  ASTEW  RAW  HASA
NEIGHBORS  SWEETHEARTS
ADORABLY  ETAL  STERILE
ADE  ALICIA  LASER
INVADERSFROMMARS
GOES  REEL  IDO  SHE
ALL  PANICINTHESTREETS
DOT  AGIN  KORAN  OAXACA
JOE  TEES  EXITS  RHYTHM
```

19 Why We Don't Go to Salad Bars with Ed

```
YES  ALAMB  STPAT    SLAP
ATT  MARIA  POOLE  WHOLE
WHATSDISH  AMPAS  ROWAN
NETH  LETTUCESITDOWN
SLUICES    REDO    ONTOP
 SEEN   ENDIVERIGHTIN
  UNHASPS   SEMI  WEEPY
AVA  UNTO   ORIANA    SEC
PEPPERNAPKIN     LAYS
ARRAS  REIN  WATT   AMAS
IDONTHAVEMUSHROOMLEFT
NINA  ONES   SHOR   AERIE
  MIRO    CAESARCOMING
SSM  NAMATH   AYAH    TEO
UNITS  ISHE  FISHIER
ROMAINESEATED    PAUL
 BIRDY   JPAT    FLANNEL
 CHEESEONHERWAY   URSA
PIKER  ALIEN  CHICKPEAS
FREES  RINSE  MONET   AGE
CARL   IATSE  PATES   DER
```

20 This 'n' That

```
AGAPE  PAPAS   BASE   MEDI
RIVAL  ITINA   AGEE   IVAN
FRANKNSTEIN  HACKNSACK
SOLD  RAYSNTOAST  EDDIE
 ORANG   ERIK   REREAD
CADRE   ELDER   ELIDE
ALEAF  SNEE  STEPNWOLF
POS  USC  MEARA  GEO  TIA
PECKNPAW  PROBE  STATEN
 EDAMES   KURALT  CONN
SCANS  PEEKNEASE  MESSY
HOLY   HIPPOS   SETTER
ORTAKE  SATAN  LOWNBROW
OFA  EAR  LOWER  FAO  ALA
KURTNRODS  TIFF   THIGH
 ROYCE   ICHOR   TONAL
MOBILE  LANA   EIEIO
OMANI  WOKNSTICKS  KNEE
RACKNTOUR  PINKNSHEERS
SHOE  ORSO  ANGLO  ORALS
EAST  PEEN  RESEW  OSTEO
```

21 You Don't Say!

```
PARA   WISPS   DRU  FLA
EXEC  PESTLE  NUPTUALS
RESTRANTEUR  ASTERICKS
 EINS  HAT   TONY   OIL
 TRIATHALON  ALI  LADY
SAV   EATS  EXCETERA
PROBBLY   SMEAR  VARGAS
CORALSEA  CODS  HEIGHTH
ATEST  SUMO   TWO  NEATO
 ISA  NORSE  ERAS  NYC
PRES  VETINARIANS  BASK
LOX  FAME  SWISS   USA
AGAPE  IMP  CHEF  ANDTO
NUCULAR  REBA  LIBATION
TETRIS  ROLLS  FEBUARY
 EXPRESSO  CAEN    LAX
GALE   ATE  COOPDEGRAH
URI  COCO   PAP  FIAT
TEMPACHUR  DETERIATING
 ANARTICA  ARENOT  INIT
 STP  SHY  PADDY   OGLE
```

22 Repeat Performance

```
ISAAC   MEDGAR   ADZ  FIN
SELDOM  OVERDO   MOE  AXE
ARSENIOOOOOOOHALL   CTS
TAO  TAN  EDW  ANTIBIAS
 NEMEA   ATOMS   GRAPE
HIYOSILVERAWAAAY  ALAN
ISART  BOY  LON  GODS
REWASH  WELLEXCUUUSEME
TEN   AISLE   HERB   LAW
 COLL   ACCEDE   LAINE
RRRUFFLESHAVERRRIDGES
UHURA   THELIP   OONA
SEL  GAME   AETNA   LED
HEEEERESJOHNNY  DREAMY
 OSLO  OMO   DRU  ERNIE
BASS  OWWWNOTSOHAAAARD
ANTIC   ILIKE   SANCT
HYPNOSIS  PSI  UGH  ASP
AWE  THTHTHATSALLFOLKS
MAT  TOE  RESEND  OODLES
AYE  ATM  INSETS   RESET
```

23 Taking Orders

```
POPSITUP  STOW  SAM  MAX
EXITLINE  LOLA  ANY  ALI
NOCREDITCARDS  PORTMAN
 IDE   RASP  NOPARKING
SNIP  NOSHIRTNOSHOES
NOSERVICE  DEBAR
ONT  SINKIN  NANO  PENTA
BEHAVE  SNARED  CILIUM
SWAMP    ROW  FALCONRY
 STASH  NORESERVATIONS
 AREA      ROAR
NOSUBSTITUTING   ALTAR
ONETOTEN  NUS    HONED
OTTAWA   SITUPS  RATEDR
NOAHS  PLOT  PALLAS  MAA
 ROBED   NOSHARING
WAITTOBESEATED   ACTS
PAYSERVER  ETRE   DUG
INATREE  ENJOYYOURMEAL
SEN  SKI  SEAM  ELEGANCE
ASK  EST  TOYS  DETENTES
```

24 A Hard-Driving Puzzle

```
PIGGISH  BANANA  MAMMAL
LORELEI  IDIDIT  AVOICE
UNINKED  BANDLEADERGUY
SIDEA   SLYE    IER  NAT
FACT  HOPI   FLIRT  VOTE
ONO  TYPEOFFRENCHWINE
USA  EPIC  ALANFREED
REC  DENT  SANTEE  LAKME
SAHL  SERF   ORWELLIAN
 VEY  SALAAM  SEN  NCO
ABIDES  LOMBARD  LODGES
PAN  SAP  PAPERS   WAD
PICTOGRAM  PITT   HOSP
TOERR  EMAJOR  PEEL  MAR
 INSTITUTE  DRNO   ONE
CROOKEDESTSTREET   FDA
CHAS  INERT   RIOT  DIRK
RUT  PPD   COUP   TITAN
ACTRESSCAROLE  APARADE
SHALLI  AWARDS  SINGLES
SUNSET  NEWEST  HASEYES
```

25 Rodents' Gallery

```
BIRCH   MAMA        STEPS
DOTHERATTHING     ARNIE
SUPERVOLESUNDAE   MAGNA
AKIN    VET   BISE   PIER
GEE  ARIA  ISL  PLO   NNE
  ANOTHERMOUSETOFEED
 WALDOS   GOPHERCOFFEE
FANCY  ALONSO  TIN  ORDO
ARNO  ALA    AAA   PRELL
BEAVERLYHILLS   LAO  DEE
  ELF   SITUATE    RLS
IFA  ASP  LEMMINGCOOKIE
MASON  EAT    ZOO   NABS
ANSA  DDS  HELIOS  JANIS
 NOTBYAHAIRON   SAUTES
 MYCHINNYCHINCHILLA
OBI  BET  AOK  APSE   MAJ
ORAL  SIAM  DLI     POGO
LITUP  CHEWIESGERBILEE
ACENT    ARMANDHAMSTER
HEDDA    ASMY    TUNAS
```

26 By the Sea, By the Sea

```
SISENOR   UPSIDE   PASTA
ANILINE  ASALOON   OSCAR
SMALLCLAMSCOURT   PSALM
SEMI   REWIRE   MER  ELKO
   SUEANN    SHE  OSTLER
SIS  MDS  OYSTERFEW   ORY
OCTOPIED   OTRA   AGASP
HEARST   OFHEAVEN  PUPAL
ORBS   FRIO   PENTA   ZONE
   ISBRIGHT   GARDYLOO
AER  PRESSONSNAILS   LNG
PROFANED    THEGLOOM
OLGA  OZAWA  IVES   RHAP
DEERE  EYELINER   FLEECE
 RRRRR  RUST  SQUIDROW
WSW  MUSSELTOV  ULE   DWS
REHEAT   IAL   IMELDA
IRES   SEP   LAXALT  SHIP
SILTY  THEOUTERLIMPETS
TAKER  NONAGON  EMPIRES
SLOES   ANDSEE  DESCENT
```

27 Maim That Tune!

```
ATA  ISHI   ADO    ESSEN
SORETHUMB  IDUB  LATVIA
POLICEHELPMEIMFALLING
SLOTHS   OAF  JARS    TOE
  HEAVINGONAJETPLANE
MARES  ENDORA    DIRE
APER  NED    PAR  COARSE
ORD  MARYHADALEGOFLAMB
16TUMS   ERA   FAA   BIB
 ILE  ALLYN   CUB   GATS
 KILLINGMESOFTLYWITH
SENT  TOA  SOLES    FIG
TEA   STY  LII   HISSAW
IFIONLYHADDENEUVE  CHI
REDSEA  AMI   ARE   AMEN
 SATE   OSKARS   BREWS
 IWRITETHESONGSTHAT
SHA   STAT   GEO   ANITAS
MAKETHEWHOLEWORLDSICK
STEREO  NANA  NICTITATE
ASNEW    NOD   LAST   SID
```

28 Wordcurrents

```
MODISTE     ATRABILIOUS
ABINTRA    ENRICOCARUSO
VISCOUS  UNDEREDUCATED
 CONSTANTINE     ESSES
STAGES  EDICT   MEOW
TERNS  SNORE  HADDIBSON
ANDI   SCENE  JARDINIERE
BEET   ERIE  CURLINGTEAM
STROPPED  BARBIE   SINCE
   ETE  BURGUNDY   NOLA
MISCUE  JESTERS  ALGREN
INCH  TRASHING   HMO
STOAT  ENTERS  REMNANTS
COLLAPSIBLE   MERE  SOHO
UNDERRATES   COLOR  THEO
TESTPILOT   BASIN  CRAFT
  AGER   LANCE  BOOSTS
HAIKU    LORDOFLORDS
UNTILTOMORROW  INSOLES
STATIONOWNER   SEEMEST
HELENMORGAN    ATTESTS
```

29 Once Upon an Island

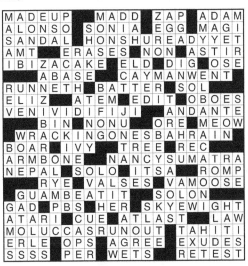

```
MADEUP   MADD  ZAP  ADAM
ALONSO   SONIA  EGG  MAGI
SANDAL  HONSHUREADYYET
AMT   ERASES   NON  ASTIR
IBIZACAKE  ELD  DIG   OSE
 ABASE    CAYMANWENT
RUNNETH  BATTER    SOL
ELIZ  ATEM  EDIT   OBOES
VENIVIDIFIJI   ANDANTE
 BIN  NONU   ORE   MEOW
 WRACKINGONESBAHRAIN
BOAR  IVY   TREE    REC
ARMBONE   NANCYSUMATRA
NEPAL  SOLO  ITSA   ROMP
 RYE  VALSES   VAMOOSE
 GUAMBEATIT    SOLON
GAD  PBS  HER  SKYEWIGHT
ATARI  CUE  ATLAST   LAW
MOLUCCASRUNOUT  TAHITI
ERLE  OPS  AGREE  EXUDES
SSSS   PER  WETS  RETEST
```

30 On the Lamb

```
EMIRS    BASSI   ACNE  ABC
DEBIT   HOTTUB  CHOY   HER
ITSPASTUREBEDTIME   ELI
TOE  RUSTING   EERO  DAVE
HONKER   AOUDADPOORDAD
  EDGAR   MEL    DUN
OBEY  ELENI  ROPO   SOSAD
LAW  HOOVESONFIRST   HOO
ELEMENT  VCR  FEST   PERU
SOC    LEAPS   ROE   APTB
THANKSFORSHEARINGTHAT
RAID  ORB  TEASE    ATE
UNDO  FIAT  ULT  PAPYRUS
SOI  MAATHEMAATICS   DRT
TITLE  REED  BROTH  NYNY
  IAM  TIS   THUMB
PLENTYOMUTTON    RICHER
HULK  AFAR  ICEPICK   ELO
OXO  RUMINANTWITHAVIEW
TOP  INAN  STEELE  DONNA
ORE  MTNS  ISTLE   OCEAN
```

31 At the Costume Ball There Was ...

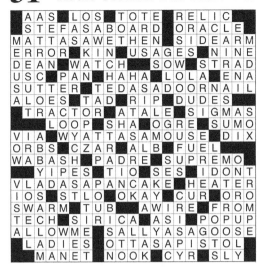

32 Final X-am

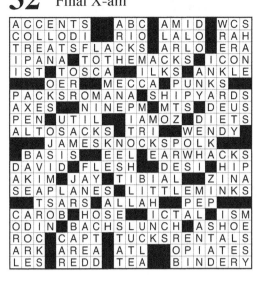

33 Film Criticism Made Simple

34 Just a Super Guy

35 Just a Super Guy, Too

36 Let's Go to the Videotape

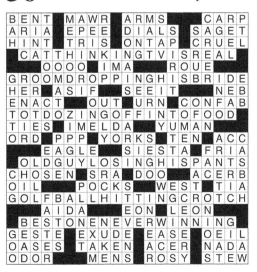

37 Hello, I Must Be Going

```
MATH  CLEAT  ABE   GREBE
ECHO  HORNE  GIN   REBECS
THELMAANDLOUSE      ADELLE
SENDOFF       PETMONDRIAN
    YIPE  HAMS  RID      EIS
PAST     SABU    JOEDEVIVRE
ISL  ANKLES  USS  ROSES
CHANREACTION      PALM
   NIKITA  CRI  LISA   SLA
LODZ   LEEJ  CONOPERATED
IDEAS    SAW  REV   EVADE
NORMANMALER   BEAM  INAN
ARS  LEAR  ANA  ISOBAR
   PLAN   PANINTHENECK
ATOOT   AJO  INVEST   SUE
FREDWONTON   STAR    PITY
IRA   ATA  LEON  OPUS
FINGERPANTS      INERTIA
EVERSO  INSURANCECLAMS
SECANT  NEA  ALBAN  INIT
  SKYES  SSR  GLAND  ETTA
```

38 Space Exploration II

```
CLASSA  BEET  LEMS  WATT
COPIED  UTAH  ARIA  ELEA
CLINTONGORE   MENDICANT
PANG  NUB   BRAINDRAIN
  SLALOM  ADS   ELAN
CURTAILMENTS    ASE  TACH
DROOL    BAY   MIO  IGLOO
IGO  ALF  DUMBARTONOAKS
MENSWEAR   IAM  AFT  NET
  DEL  ANO  IDLES  TRE
   YOUNGMANWITHAHORN
   END  ELGIN  AGE  TUM
ISM  DEE  OOF  GASPEDAL
THECARPENTERS   REO  GNU
REALM  IVE   TAG  KLEES
YALU  ACE  THEGOODEARTH
  BABA  WOO  STUART
MISFORMING   ICK   TIME
COLORADAN  GOONHOLIDAY
HOLD  RING  EXIT  TACOMA
ESSA  DAYS  DODO  ADELES
```

39 Subliminal Chess

```
ACH  TEATIME  DOME  OWOE
SHOPAWNINGS  IDEA  ZEST
MARQUEENAME  GILGAMESH
USERS   GNU  MIN  LEAKIN
DEBS  ALL  ATIT  DER  NEO
  TAXIED  ASSAY  OBI
ACT  REB  ATKA  PEA  EGGO
BROOKLYNBRIDGE   METHOD
COMP  SAO  ANDA  PALETTE
SPEED  BIGG  RHETT  SOS
  DRIVINGAMBITION
PER  AVAST  COOL   NOBEL
INASPOT  ECHO  DOS  TODO
NOBLER  BROADCASTLINGO
ELBA  YES  ONYX  TAO  YEN
  IMP  MAGIC  ICETUB
PAS  UNU  ANET  NOS  AURA
ASHORE  ORG  ELI  ABBOT
STORESIGN  APINTOFYOUR
TOPE  TORE  BESTALEMATE
ARES  SUET  RETHREW  TEE
```

40 Gag Orders

```
 BELLE  ISSY  PPS  CANT
SENIOR  MAYO  IRA  ALOHA
WAITUNTILSUPPER  SAHIB
ING  SOOT  TAKEFIVE  ESE
LIMA   JAM  RST  ASSAIL
LEARNTOTYPE  TROT  RVS
  TOO  EEL  GEOM  LOYAL
AGR  WAD  YODA  ANTE  LSD
LIE  DIVEDIVEDIVE  ITS
PVTS  SEE  NIT   SCIFI
SEUSS  THISENDUP  HATCH
 MRMOM  COS  SEA  NIKE
PEN  MOREICECREAM  NUN
HAT  MEAL  KNEE  RAG  GPS
ICOME  TKOS  RAF  ZAP
 RSA  WEEP  SAILWESTMEN
NEEDLE  PIT  RAW  AYLI
OWN  IBEFOREE  PIKE  LIN
MCDIV  LESSPULPINTHEOJ
SUEDE  ATE  TREE  ERRATA
 TROD  LAD  OOID  WEEDS
```

41 Keep It Clean

```
 WASI  TMS  ISM  INFER
GOLAN  RIEN  DUI  NORSE
MONEYLAUNDERERS  CREME
WATCHESTHESOAPS  AIDED
APB  ITCH  RTE  LENSED
HEEP  ESL  JUDO  GROG
  RAIN  OTTERS  STAYON
 THEBLEACHERS  AMI  EPA
PRICES  TURNS  ARAM  RST
SAFER  IOTON  SMILER
IDIDNTKNOWITWASLOADED
  EARNER  SEIZE  FREYA
CAW  TEES  SALVE  ADELEH
HHH  HAW  CYCLESAVAGES
EMILYS  BOREAL  GAYE
ZETA  OPUS  SHO  MRED
 EVENAS  DOO  EROO  EMU
HEWED  THEVERYFABRICOF
ATARI  AMERICANSOCIETY
HASNT  KAL  LAME  LUISE
ASHES  INS   SSR  ITIS
```

42 Anything Goes

```
OEDIPUSREX  APIAN  POMP
PREVENTIVE  GORGO  OREL
INCENTIVES  ALOES  LENA
EEK  ARLES  GRINS  BALDY
  KNELT  GRITS  SENSES
SENEGAL  PEACE  CHASED
EXIT  TIGERS  STMARK
TENT  EFLATS  SAIL  IST
PRELUDEINF  CERNAN  MAS
OTTER  BURGH  PULI  ARM
III  GOB  TOPAR  SAX  SKI
NOE  EXAM  BORES  ETHER
TNT  SCRAPE  TOOKADRINK
 SHE  AGUA  CRISIS  ANTE
 SHREDS  SOLOLP  ITOR
NOPETS  TYPOS  GASTONS
MOURNS  CREAM  PANTS
ESTES  DAYAN  TALIA  JET
AIRS  SERBS  COLLARBONE
DEUS  EATAT  UPPERVOLTA
ERNO  ELEGY  POINDEXTER
```

43 — The Lost Films of Jerry Lewis

```
OTIS WRENS BARE OGLE
WANT ENVOI ADEN GEOS
NUTANDJEFF BARTLETTS
EGOS NUTTYMARIETTA
CANNER CENSOR NAM YAY
IPUT IOUS MUS IBM
NET NEXTTONUTTIN ANTS
EMK AGEE PUSHED FRUIT
MAILMAN HATH RICO TRY
ANNIE BURR ONOUR TEX
GETTHEETOANUTTERY
SEC AREAS CRUM WEBBS
OXO GARR TKOS PROCURE
WILTS OCEANA MOOR MOD
STEW ANUTTERWORLD PGA
OKD BET INTL SPAN
ASS ADA RELENT BATONS
NUTDESCENDING VASE
SCARLATTI ASTAIRCASE
ERIN LOTT RUINS OMIT
LENO TRAY SEPIA TYPE
```

44 — Double Bills, the Sequel

```
LONE DICE GUAVAS
TENARMEDANDDANGEROUS
WHENWORLDSCOLLIDEBOOM
ORDAIN EMITS INA FOE
NEG NOS ISH MSG ELAND
ORES IOU ROOT ETA
THEDAMNEDNEIGHBORS
THRALLS OED DRAY PEA
IRE VEE BOSSA ILL ESP
COLSON ALI BUS GNU
HUDSCANDAL MASHTHEFLY
PST EON ABE HAMITE
LEW AFT COMMA MEG REP
IRA BLOC SIB SUGARED
PSYCHOPATHSOFGLORY
HOP NEAT UTE ELAM
OLDER TNT RAN SIP ELI
ROE WHO RENTA COTTEN
BURNTHETOASTOFNEWYORK
DRIVINGMISSDAISYNUTS
PATIOS YORE SETS
```

45 — Woofgang

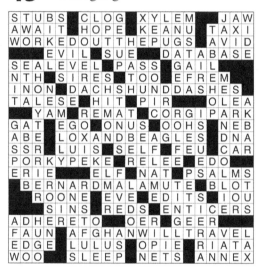

```
STUBS CLOG XYLEM JAW
AWAIT HOPE KEANU TAXI
WORKEDOUTTHEPUGS AVID
EVIL SUE DATABASE
SEALEVEL PASS GAIL
NTH SIRES TOO EFREM
INON DACHSHUNDDASHES
TALESE HIT PIR OLEA
YAM REMAT CORGIPARK
GAT EGO ONUS OOHS NEB
ABE LOXANDBEAGLES DNA
SSR LUIS SELF FEU CAR
PORKYPEKE RELEE EDO
ERIE ELF NAT PSALMS
BERNARDMALAMUTE BLOT
ROONE EVE EDITS IOU
SINS REDS ENTICERS
ADHERETO OER GEER
FAUN AFGHANWILLTRAVEL
EDGE LULUS OPIE RIATA
WOO SLEEP NETS ANNEX
```

46 — Fashion Your Seat Belts

```
FFFF THROAT OBOE CHAT
ELLA WEARWITHALL HERB
LEARNINGTHEROBES ARCS
TAXMAN SODA AGITPROP
ISIS YMA EEL
LEPER NODRESSPASSING
AXEL MANIA TAN SNORE
LETYOURGARBDOWN VIA
ORD STUS ALE ATLEAST
TOPMASTS OBIT RAT
CLOTHESBUTNOCIGAR
USE REOS PERCALES
ALAMEDA LEO BIOS DES
TAR SUITSFROMTHEHIP
MICRO TRA SOAPS TOJO
CHANGINGATTIRE GETIT
NEO OLA DRAM
TOSTADAS FLAG GEORGE
ANTE APPARELOFMONKEYS
SCAR RAIMENTBRRR RAMS
KEYS DRNO TOYOTA ALSO
```

47 — 2B or Not 2B

```
CAPS NASH ABS VANE
OLIO OREO SLAT SAXON
MONO CENT GABBYTALESE
BETTYANDBARNEYRULE
OSO ONA ANODES LETUP
MUD ETNA ALS RED
QUEENOFTHENIBBLE SITE
USING LOS FAIL OHARA
OHGO SAN RUINGALCOHOL
TEETHE SPIN GONETO
ARR EVA HOTEL SHE CAS
PRESTO IVES ATBEST
PIGEONHOBBLE CAR ALTO
ASOLD RAII OOH OCEAN
RAFT MADABOUTTHEBOBBY
KAA GYM LOOT YON
CRAIG CHIEFS DEE FDA
CLUBBINGACROSSWORD
FRUITYPELES OUZO ALIA
HERDS ORTS PIER XING
AXIS ESS ENDE YOKE
```

48 — Palindromania

```
EFREM LEI BASSO FALA
LLAMAMALL ARGUER ITIS
LATEXETAL TOOFATAFOOT
AGER RINSES SEVENTH
GWEN SET TIGE ETA
RMS ILSA TARARAARARAT
OPENLY VIE ATA STP
TAMED CAVEGIRL ASST
CAINAMONOMANIAC DIANA
DESERT BEA APILLAR
SDI SENILEFELINES APT
COMPETE ONE MARAUD
AREAS DRATSUCHCUSTARD
ROSY EDITSOUT TALER
UNK LUC ERR BEHAVE
STEPONNOPETS TERR SSW
OHS LEOG DRU LISA
RETAILS OPINED TASK
TOILETELIOT NAGAPAGAN
IRMA OTITIS EMILSLIME
EYED NOBEL ZEE TENSE
```

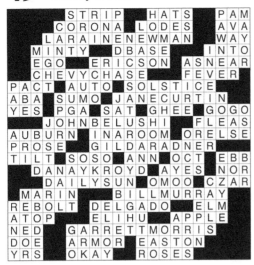

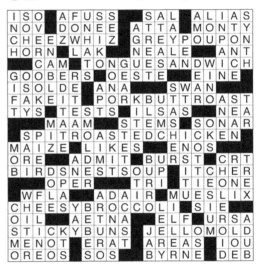

55 Our Crowded Cities

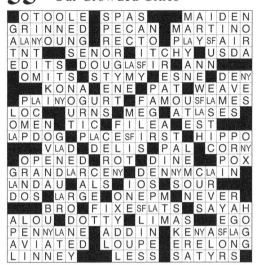

56 Word Salad, Chunky-Style

57 Special Delivery

58 Oktoberfest

59 Leveling the Playing Field

60 Final Ballot

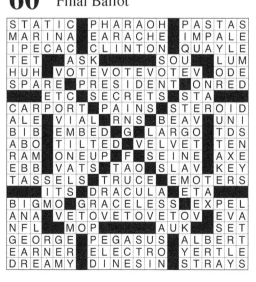

Hurricane 1 Solution

INWARD: decal, Perseus, Sinai, latinos, massage, drag, Derek, Cordelia, red nose, Borgnine, Vespucci, hairy, Stella, beta, minarets, bolder.

OUTWARD: Red Lobster, animate, ballet, Syria, hiccups, evening, Robeson, derailed, rocker, Edgar Degas, Samson, Italian, issues, replaced.

Hurricane 2 Solution

INWARD: meets, engine, begat, love note, casino, day care, till, Israel, laminate, bitten, Al Pacino, revenue, jelly, remained, ragamuffins.

OUTWARD: sniff, Uma, gardenia, Meryl, Lejeune, Veronica, planet, Tibetan, "I'm all ears," illiteracy, Adonis, acetone, voltage, benign, esteem.

Hurricane 3 Solution

INWARD: Stradivari, Giuliani, serif, Simenon, alumni, rips apart, tar pit, Qatar, tsetse, Dali, attach, Torre, Beulah, torte, Byrne, Hot Lips.

OUTWARD: spilt, O. Henry, betrothal, Ueberroth, cattail, Adeste, strata, Q-tip, rat-trap, Aspirin, Mulan, one, misfire, Sinai, Luigi, Ravi, darts.

Hurricane 4 Solution

INWARD: semantic, Illini, peninsula, dead air, a la mode, protoplasm, layer, Gena, Zyrtec, integrates, Palermo, snarl at, ipso, havoc, Cabot.

OUTWARD: tobacco, VA hospital, ransom, relapse, target, "nice try," Zane Grey, alms, Alpo, torpedo, malaria, Daedalus, ninepin, illicit, names.

Hurricane 5 Solution

INWARD: retinues, saver, cognates, in a draw, desserts, maestros, afoot, Tokyo, brat, laymen, Elaine May, a la, B major, Ella, backlist, Carter.

OUTWARD: retract, silk, caballero, jambalaya, menial, enemy, altar boy, Kotto, of a sort, seamstress, Edward, anise, tango, crevasse, uniter.

Do You Have "Puzzling" Friends or Relatives?
Give the Gift that Keeps Them That Way!

ORDER FORM
(*** PLEASE PRINT CLEARLY ***)

Your Name _____

Address _____

City/State/Zip _____

Phone (optional) (_____) _____ - _____

Recipient (if a gift) _____

Address _____

City/State/Zip _____

(Other recipients may be listed on the back.)

			Quantity	Subtotal
Best of Merl, Book 2		$14		
Best of Merl, Book 1		$14		
Merl Reagle's 100th Anniv. Puzzle Book		$14		
Merl Reagle's Sunday Crosswords	Vol. 18	$12		
	Vol. 17	$12		
	Vol. 16	$12		
	Vol. 15	$12		
	Vol. 14	$12		
	Vol. 12	$12		
	Vol. 11	$12		
	Vol. 10	$12		
	Vol. 9	$12		
	Vol. 8	$12		
	Vol. 4	$12		
	Vol. 3	$12		
	Vol. 2	$12		
	Vol. 1	$12		

FINAL TOTAL $_____

Send check or money order (payable to "The PuzzleWorks") to:
CROSSWORDS, P.O. BOX 15066, TAMPA FL 33684-5066.

ORDER FORM
(*** PLEASE PRINT CLEARLY ***)

Your Name _____

Address _____

City/State/Zip _____

Phone (optional) (_____) _____ - _____

Recipient (if a gift) _____

Address _____

City/State/Zip _____

(Other recipients may be listed on the back.)

			Quantity	Subtotal
Best of Merl, Book 2		$14		
Best of Merl, Book 1		$14		
Merl Reagle's 100th Anniv. Puzzle Book		$14		
Merl Reagle's Sunday Crosswords	Vol. 18	$12		
	Vol. 17	$12		
	Vol. 16	$12		
	Vol. 15	$12		
	Vol. 14	$12		
	Vol. 12	$12		
	Vol. 11	$12		
	Vol. 10	$12		
	Vol. 9	$12		
	Vol. 8	$12		
	Vol. 4	$12		
	Vol. 3	$12		
	Vol. 2	$12		
	Vol. 1	$12		

FINAL TOTAL $_____

Send check or money order (payable to "The PuzzleWorks") to:
CROSSWORDS, P.O. BOX 15066, TAMPA FL 33684-5066.

Send all correspondence and orders to:

The PuzzleWorks
P.O. Box 15066
Tampa FL 33684-5066

Or visit our website at www.sundaycrosswords.com